D0113841

Reliving the Passion

Books by Walter Wangerin Jr.

The Book of God:
The Bible as a Novel

Paul: A Novel

Saint Julian

The Book of the Dun Cow

The Book of Sorrows

The Crying for a Vision

This Earthly Pilgrimage

Little Lamb, Who Made Thee?

The Manger Is Empty

Miz Lil and the Chronicles
of Grace

Ragman and Other Cries
of Faith

In the Days of the Angels

Preparing for Jesus

Reliving the Passion

Whole Prayer

Father and Son

Mourning into Dancing

The Orphean Passages

As for Me and My House

For Children

Mary's First Christmas

Peter's First Easter

The Book of God for Children

Probity Jones and
the Fear-Not Angel

Thistle

Potter

In the Beginning There
Was No Sky

Angels and All Children

Water, Come Down

The Bedtime Rhyme

Swallowing the Golden Stone

Branta and the Golden Stone

Elisabeth and the Water Troll

WALTER
WANGERIN JR.

Reliving the Passion

Meditations
on the
Suffering,
Death,
and
Resurrection
of Jesus
as Recorded
in Mark

ZONDERVAN

ZONDERVAN.com/
AUTHORTRACKER
follow your favorite authors

ZONDERVAN

Reliving the Passion
Copyright © 1992 by Walter Wangerin, Jr.

Requests for information should be addressed to:

Zondervan, *Grand Rapids, Michigan 49530*

Library of Congress Cataloging-in-Publication Data

Wangerin, Walter.
     Reliving the passion : meditations on the suffering, death, and resurrection
of Jesus as recorded in Mark / Walter Wangerin, Jr.
        p.   cm.
     ISBN 978-0-310-75530-2
     1. Jesus Christ—Passion—and devotion—English 2. Lent—Prayer-books and
devotions—English. I. Title.
BT431.W35   1992
232.96—dc20   91-32854

Published in association with Alive Communications, Inc., 7680 Goddard Street,
Suite 200, Colorado Springs, CO 80920. www.alivecommunications.com

Printed in the United States of America

10 11 12 13 14 15 16 • 30 29 28 27 26 25 24 23 22 21 20 19 18 17 16 15

For Walter Pieper
whose friendship
permitted me the time
and the freedom
to meditate

CONTENTS

Reliving the Passion

PREFACE

I LOVE YOU, LORD JESUS

In the sincerest silence of my soul, I murmured over and over, "I love you, Lord Jesus."

Jesus was dying. I could do nothing to save him—not even to ease him. I could only watch and suffer the sorrow too. I was a child. Yet I saw every detail of his passion exactly as the Bible set it down. Everything. I learned everything. Not because I was precocious, but because I *felt* it all.

And always there came the moment when I burst into tears.

Jesus looked at me. The love in his face was so horrible that I started to cry, and I murmured over and over, "I love you, too! I love you, Lord Jesus."

Did he hear me? At the moment I couldn't know, because he was dying.

Now I know.

He heard me.

† † †

In those days my father was the pastor of a modest church in North Dakota. I was his eldest son, an earnest child, wide-eyed by nature, and watchful. The name of the church was Immanuel, "God With Us": I believed that. The interior of the church building was bare brick painted white. In the evenings, when the windows were blackened by night, the white walls softened to an incandescent orange, and the whole building

11

became a place of consolations, a familiar fortress wherein I was safe from the evil without. In the evenings, then, I relaxed my guard. I allowed my imagination considerable freedom.

And on Wednesday evenings, late in winter, for a full six weeks preceding Easter, my father preached of the passions of Jesus.

These were our Lenten services.

His sermons were dramatic. He would assume the character of a disciple, Peter denying the Christ, John leading the mother of Jesus away, Mary Magdalene watching from a distance. Perhaps this form of discourse trained me and translated me (in spirit) to the time of Christ itself, just as great art always persuades us to experience the thing it presents. Perhaps because my imagination was safe in a golden fortress it was quicker to dart inside a story and to live there. Whatever the causes, when my father took the Bible on Wednesday evenings and began to read of the sorrows of Jesus—from the Last Supper to his last cry on the cross—I was there.

That's why I cried.

The reading made real the story—so terribly real to a boy of eight that I was swept through the events of the Gospel not as though recalling them, but feeling them in fact.

Is it in hearing that faith begins? Yes. And is faith an intimate, real relationship with Jesus? Yes. And this is the strength of our sacred story, that when we hear it we experience it; and in the experience we meet the Christ; and him whom we meet in the extremes of his love, we must likewise love.

So my father was reading the Bible while the winds of winter shrieked outside; but I wasn't in the white-brick church. I was nowhere in North Dakota. I had slipped into The Story. . . .

† † †

Teeth. I saw teeth before me.

Teeth: in Gethsemane Judas was grinning with teeth as big as tombstones. Torchlight flashed in his eye, false laughter. He kissed the Lord Jesus. I shivered.

Then the High Priest was clashing his teeth together, hissing horribly, "Blassssphemy!"

Ugly men spat on the Lord through crumbling teeth. But Jesus stood cool and silent: the Christ, as calm as the white candle—and its single flame—tall by the altar in Immanuel. I gazed at his patience, and I grieved.

Teeth: Pontius Pilate had piggy-little teeth. The multitude gnashed ratchet teeth of violence, crying, "Crucify him!" Pilate simpered and surrendered, dipping the tips of his fingers in water. I wanted to cry. Jesus didn't even open his mouth. I never saw his teeth. He was different from them all. He was different from me, because I would have cursed the people.

We walked to Golgotha, that hollow head in the hillside. I saw the sweating faces of soldiers as they set spikes to my master's hands—but I couldn't look at his face. I shut my eyes.

My father was reading: *And when they crucified him—*

I heard a gasp as they lifted the Lord aloft.

Then, when I opened my eyes, I was astounded by a change. Suddenly I was seeing everything as Jesus saw it. I was (we were) looking down on the sea of faces, twisted faces, brown teeth, broken teeth, jeering at Jesus, crying him down from the cross. I heard him groan by my ear.

In my heart I said, *Let's get out of here! Please, let's go.*

These people were purple with hatred. Women and men and soldiers and slaves, the teachers, the leaders, their faces enraged. The loathing rose in waves around us, and I pleaded, *Please, let's go away! Let's go!*

But Jesus was different, not like me. "Father, forgive them," he whispered. "They know not what they do."

I felt the bones beside me, no motion but the crack of his hanging. I heard his purposeful breathing by my ear and, with a sort of horror, realized he wasn't going anywhere. He was choosing to stay right here.

Then the thief on our left began to bellow, "Let's get out of here. Let's go! If you're the Christ, get down from the cross and take me too. Let's go! Let's go!"

I felt ill. I felt so guilty. That sinner was speaking my words out loud! I decided to say no more.

But then the thief on our right hand said, "Lord, remember me," and Jesus twisted around to look at him—

No! Jesus was looking at *me*! Things had changed again, and it was as if *I* were the one who had said, *Remember me*. To me, then, the Lord said, "Today you will be with me in Paradise."

And that is when I burst into tears.

I cried because I wasn't with him any more. I was on a different cross. We were each alone.

But I also cried because he did what he did for me! To take me to Paradise! He loved me. Jesus loved me. He looked at me, and the love was so horrible—

His arms torn up at the sockets, the weight of his body popping the armpits, the ribs pulled apart, stretching his flesh. I could count his bones! He whispered, "Today" and "Paradise," and I burst into tears, murmuring over and over, *I love you too. I love you, Lord Jesus.*

Then came a torment I did not imagine because I could not. This was something past comprehension. His chest began to heave. His body thrashed against the wood. He threw back his head and stared at the black skies, and he screamed, "My God! My God! Why hast thou forsaken me?"

Nobody answered. I couldn't stop crying.

My father was reading: *Darkness over the whole land until the ninth hour—*

Out of that darkness there suddenly came the roaring of his voice, an inarticulate scream, a wild and final cry. And then he died. I saw his head slump forward. I saw the chin fall to his chest. I heard the air go out. I saw his body sag. I was sad. I was so sad.

In the night of Good Friday, my father was reading: *He gave up the ghost. And the veil of the temple was rent in twain—*

By then it was not winter in North Dakota any more. Neither was it spring. It was bleak hell. My father was wearing a

14

black robe only. The altar had been stripped of linen. All things were sad, all things severe and dark and dark and very true.

And the preacher said, "He died for you."

How was I supposed to feel at that? Guilty? Beloved?

Jesus, I was just a child then. I loved you with an incomprehensible pain. I did not want you to be dead.

Jesus?

Dear Lord Jesus—do you know what a whooping joy I felt when my father read the rest of the story?

Who ran to the tomb on Sunday morning? Me! That was me! I stuck my head in the empty spaces. And when the gardener spoke, I got me a good spot next to Mary Magdalene.

And who was the gardener? Why, it was you!

To Mary you said, "Mary."

But to me you said, "Wally, I love you."

Ha ha! And I with shining eyes said, "I love you too. I love you, Lord Jesus. I do."

† † †

This is the light that has shone in our darkness—in the winters of North Dakota, in the melancholy winters of old, exhausted souls—and the darkness has not overcome it! This, then, is the way we may enter the story of Jesus, the history of our salvation, that the Gospel might in every way become our own.

To that end have I prepared the meditations of this book.

It is my intent that they should lead a reader step by step to an Easter celebration, walking with Jesus both in thought (learning along the way) and in a genuine feeling (experiencing The Way—experiencing the love of the Lord in his passion).

Forty Steps to the Journey

It is surely possible and right to take this journey to the Resurrection at any time, whenever the personal need and readiness arise.

But these forty devotions fit best the forty days that lead to Easter, one for each day (except Sundays, when public worship preempts this private practice).

Forty days has come to be an excellent period in which to prepare for the Resurrection of the Lord. Jesus took forty days in the wilderness to fast, to fight the Devil, and to prepare for his ministry. Likewise, Moses spent forty days on Mount Sinai, receiving the Law (which no one finally kept but Jesus himself). In the Old Testament a special meaning was attached to the forty-day period: devout encounter with the Lord. But then that meaning was both acknowledged and superseded in the New Testament by Christ's divine activity—and the Law was superseded by Grace!

Therefore we, in matching our own forty days of faithful commitment to the Lord's, admit the reality of Grace in our lives and mimic our Jesus as well.

Read the first meditation on the Wednesday traditionally called "Ash Wednesday." It's identified on most calendars. The fortieth day before Easter (not counting Sundays), it has marked the start of the season of Lent ever since the sixth century A.D.

In fact, as you fulfill these meditations day by day, you will be participating in an ancient practice of our Christian Church: observing Lent, examining yourself for your own deep need of Jesus' grace, understanding the crucifixion as the moment of marvelous love and your salvation, and giving God thanks for a resurrection which promises your own in the end.

Each devotion shall focus on a passage from Holy Scripture. In order to maintain a narrative unity, allowing the devotions to flow easily one from the other, I've elected to follow the passion of our Lord, verse by verse, as written in Mark's account of the Gospel.

It would be to your advantage then if, before you begin these devotions, you read the fourteenth and fifteenth chapters of Mark all in one sitting.

God be with you.

Earnestly I pray blessings upon the hours we are about to spend together—that your hearts grow young again and that, like children in sorrow, like children in joy, you finally cry in the silence of souls, *I love you, Lord Jesus. I do!*

Walter Wangerin

PROLOGUE

FOUR REASONS FOR RELIVING THE PASSION

THE FIRST DAY

ASH WEDNESDAY

LUKE 12:16–21

> And he told them a parable, saying,
>
> "The land of a rich man brought forth plentifully; and he thought to himself, 'What shall I do, for I have nowhere to store my crops?' And he said, 'I will do this: I will pull down my barns, and build larger ones; and there I will store all my grain and my goods. And I will say to my soul, Soul, you have ample goods laid up for many years; take your ease, eat, drink, be merry.'
>
> "But God said to him, 'Fool! This night your soul is required of you; and the things you have prepared, whose will they be?'
>
> "So is he who lays up treasures for himself and is not rich toward God."

Whenever the journey to Easter begins, it must always begin right here: at the contemplation of my death, in the cold conviction that I shall die.

"Remember," the Pastor has said for centuries, always on this day. "Remember," the Pastor has murmured, touching a finger to ash in a dish and smearing the ash on my forehead—

"Remember, thou art dust, and to dust thou shalt return."

Ash Wednesday, the day of the personal ashes, the first of the forty days of Lent: Like a deep bell tolling, this word defines the day and starts the season and bids me begin my devotional journey: *Memento!* "Remember!"

Well! But that sounds old in a modern ear, doesn't it? Fusty, irrelevant, and positively medieval! Why should I think about death when all the world cries "Life" and "Live"? The priests of this age urge me toward "positive thinking," "grabbing the gusto," "feeling good about myself." And didn't Jesus himself promise life in abundance? It's annoying to find the easy flow of my full life interrupted by the morbid prophecy that it shall end. Let's keep things in their places, simple and safe: life now, while there is life; death later, when there must be death. . . .

Nevertheless, *Memento!* tolls the ageless bell. In spite of my resistance, the day and the season together warn: "Remember!" And God, in Jesus' parable, interrupts my ease indeed with an insult. "Fool!" says God (and so long as it stays a parable, this is a caution; but when I shall hear it in fact, it has become a death knell). "Fool! This night your soul is required of you; and the things you have prepared, whose will they be?"

Keep it simple? says the Lord. Fool, this is as simple as it gets: if you do not interrupt your life with convictions of the death to come, then neither shall your death, when it comes, be interrupted by life. "Life now, death later," indeed! But your life will be now only, and brief. Your death will be forever.

Ancient is this warning of the church—so ancient that the modern Christian is embarrassed to find her church ignorant, contrary to the freedoms of this age. Ancient, likewise, is the season of Lent, when the Christian is encouraged to think of her death and the sin that caused it—to examine herself, to know herself so deeply and well that knowledge becomes confession. But ancient, too, is the consolation such an exercise provides, ancient precisely because it is eternal.

It is this: that when we genuinely remember the death we deserve to die, we will be moved to remember the death the Lord in fact did die—because his took the place of ours. Ah, children, we will yearn to hear the Gospel story again and again, ever seeing therein our death in his, and rejoicing that we will therefore know a rising like his as well.

Remember now that thou art dust. Death now—yes, even in the midst of a bustling life. My death and Jesus' death, by grace conjoined. *Memento!*—because this death, remembered now, yields life hereafter. And *that* life is forever.

† † †

Ah, dear Jesus!

I feel the ashes of mortality upon my heart. Give me, please, the courage to acknowledge them; then give me the faithful sight to see them on your forehead; for you have died the death in my stead, my Redeemer and my Lord!

Amen.

THE SECOND DAY
THURSDAY

ISAIAH 53:4–6
> *Surely he has borne our griefs*
>   *and carried our sorrows;*
> *yet we esteemed him stricken,*
>   *smitten by God, and afflicted.*
> *But he was wounded for our transgressions,*
>   *he was bruised for our iniquities;*
> *upon him was the chastisement that made us whole,*
>   *and with his stripes we are healed.*
> *All we like sheep have gone astray;*
>   *we have turned every one to his own way;*
> *and the Lord has laid on him*
>   *the iniquity of us all.*

In mirrors I see myself. But in mirrors made of glass and silver I never see the *whole* of myself. I see the me I want to see, and I ignore the rest.

Mirrors that hide nothing hurt me. They reveal an ugliness I'd rather deny. Yow! Avoid these mirrors of veracity!

My wife is such a mirror. When I have sinned against her, my sin appears in the suffering of her face. Her tears reflect with terrible accuracy my selfishness. My *self!* But I hate the sight, and the same selfishness I see now makes me look away.

"Stop crying!" I command, as though the mirror were at fault. Or else I just leave the room. Walk away.

Oh, what a coward I am, and what a fool! Only when I

have the courage fully to look, clearly to know myself—even the evil of myself—will I admit my need for healing. But if I look away from her whom I have hurt, I have also turned away from her who might forgive me. I reject the very source of my healing.

My denial of my sin protects, preserves, perpetuates that sin! Ugliness in me, while I live in illusions, can only grow the uglier.

Mirrors that hide nothing hurt me. But this is the hurt of purging and precious renewal—and these are mirrors of dangerous grace.

The passion of Christ, his suffering and his death, is such a mirror. Are the tears of my dear wife hard to look at? Well, the pain in the face of Jesus is harder. It is my *self* in my extremest truth. My sinful self. The death he died reflects a selfishness so extreme that by it I was divorced from God and life and light completely: I raised my *self* higher than God! But because the Lord God is the only true God, my pride did no more, in the end, than to condemn this false god of my *self* to death. For God will *be* God, and all false gods will fall before him.

So that's what I see reflected in the mirror of Christ's crucifixion: my death. My rightful punishment. My sin and its just consequence. Me. And precisely because it is so accurate, the sight is nearly intolerable.

Nevertheless, I will not avoid this mirror! No, I will carefully rehearse, again this year, the passion of my Jesus— with courage, with clarity and faith; for this is the mirror of dangerous grace, purging more purely than any other.

For this one is not made of glass and silver, nor of fallen flesh only. This mirror is made of righteous flesh and of divinity, both—and this one loves me absolutely. My wife did not choose to take my sin and so to reflect my truth to me. She was driven, poor woman. But Jesus did choose—not only to take the sin within himself, not only to reflect the squalid truth of my personal need, but also to reveal the tremendous truth of his grace and forgiveness. He took that sin *away*.

This mirror is not passive only, showing what is; it is active, creating new things to be. It shows me a new me behind the shadow of a sinner. For when I gaze at his crucifixion, I see my death indeed—but my death *done!* His death is the death of the selfish one, whom I called ugly and hated to look upon.

And resurrection is another me.

† † †

Merciful Lord,

Hold me to the fire long enough to know my whole self truly, long enough to be cleansed by your burning forgiveness. Let me feel your passion again, studiously and well, to my good and to your glory, forever.

Amen.

THE THIRD DAY
FRIDAY

MARK 14:27-28

> And Jesus said to them, "You will all fall away; for it is written, 'I will strike the shepherd, and the sheep will be scattered.' But after I am raised up, I will go before you to Galilee."

MARK 16:6-7

> And he said to them, "Do not be amazed; you seek Jesus of Nazareth, who was crucified. He has risen, he is not here; see the place where they laid him. But go, tell his disciples and Peter that he is going before you to Galilee; there you will see him, as he told you."

Twice—near the beginning and then near the end of Jesus' passion—the same promise is repeated. It receives an emphasis, then, which makes it thematic in the story itself, and so it can teach us how to approach the passion of our Lord.

I will go (he is going) before you to Galilee. That promise is both a call and a consolation.

Surely it's meant to be factual: the disciples will in fact meet the resurrected Lord in Galilee.

But since Mark is writing his Gospel for disciples of another time and another place (Christians persecuted in Rome in the latter half of the first century, people who would never see a geographic Galilee) there may lurk another, deeper meaning in the word.

"Galilee" for the Roman Christians (and for us) may refer

to the place where Jesus initiated his serious ministry—where his conflicts with the hard world first began. In "Galilee" his enemies appeared and criticized him even for healing and doing good. From this "Galilee" Jesus' itinerary was south to Judah, up to Jerusalem, where enmity hardened into persecution, up Golgotha even to the cross. Jesus' personal "going," then, was a trip through suffering and death to resurrection.

If Jesus "will go before" his disciples from Galilee as he had gone before, then this is a call to follow him down the hard road of conflict, criticism, enmity, persecution, suffering and death and resurrection. So the passion story becomes a roadmap for all of Jesus' followers (who deny themselves and take up their crosses) whether Christians martyred in the first, or Christians bold in the twentieth, centuries.

Read this story, then, as a detailed itinerary of the disciple's life.

But hear in it as well the constant consolation—not only that he, in "going before us," is always near us, however hard the persecution; but also that we, in going his way to Galilee, *will see him as he told you*. The dearest comfort in this promise is that precisely by taking the Way of the Lord, we will meet the Lord himself. In suffering is he revealed! In the experience of our own crosses is he made manifest. Exactly so were the Christian Romans consoled by Mark's Good News—the story of Jesus. Exactly so ourselves, in our more distant deserts.

"Jesus has many who love His Kingdom in Heaven," writes Thomas à Kempis in *The Imitation of Christ*, "but few who bear his Cross. Many follow Jesus to the Breaking of the Bread, but few to the drinking of the Cup of His Passion. They who love Jesus for His own sake, and not for the sake of comfort for themselves, bless Him in every trial and anguish of heart, no less than in the greatest joy."

Be cross-bearers, then. These are the truer followers.

From Galilee to Golgotha: first we study the map, the Passion; and then—actually traveling the passionate path ourselves, "going" even as we were called—we will see him too, just as he promised we would.

† † †

Master,

Grant me, in the study of your story, both love and faith. Love will make me attentive to all you do. Faith will make me bold to follow you. I beg to see you, O my Savior!

Amen.

THE FOURTH DAY
SATURDAY

JOHN 16:20–22

"Truly, truly, I say to you, you will weep and lament, but the world will rejoice; you will be sorrowful, but your sorrow will turn into joy. When a woman is in travail she has sorrow, because her hour has come; but when she is delivered of the child, she no longer remembers the anguish, for joy that a child is born into the world.

"So you have sorrow now, but I will see you again and your hearts will rejoice, and no one will take your joy from you."

JOHN 20:19b–20

Jesus came and stood among them and said to them, "Peace be with you." When he had said this, he showed them his hands and his side. Then the disciples were glad when they saw the Lord.

So then, in three days we have counted three good reasons for reliving the passion of our Lord:

Ashes: it is necessary now to remember death, our own and our Savior's.

The mirror: it is right to recognize our sin as the cause of death, to see in Christ's story our sorrier selves and our need of his holy self.

The roadmap: it is expedient to study the Way by which all his disciples must follow him, and to receive the promise of a personal meeting with Christ on the Way.

There is yet a fourth good reason: that we prepare for joy.

The difference between shallow happiness and a deep, sustaining joy is sorrow. Happiness lives where sorrow is not. When sorrow arrives, happiness dies. It can't stand pain. Joy, on the other hand, rises from sorrow and therefore can withstand all grief. Joy, by the grace of God, is the transfiguration of suffering into endurance, and of endurance into character, and of character into hope—and the hope that has become our joy does not (as happiness must for those who depend upon it) disappoint us.

In the sorrows of the Christ—as we ourselves experience them—we prepare for Easter, for joy. There can be no resurrection from the dead except first there is a death! But then, because we love him above all things, his rising *is* our joy. And then the certain hope of our own resurrection warrants the joy both now and forever.

For the moment, lay yourselves aside. Become one of the first disciples. And in that skin, consider: what makes the appearance of the resurrected Lord such a transport of joy for you? Consider this in every fiber of your created being. How is it that so durable a joy is born at this encounter?—joy that shall hereafter survive threats and dangers and persecutions, confusions and death, even your own death?

Well, Jesus has been dead. Now he is alive. No one expects the dead to live. This causes a speechless astonishment. Is this also joy?

Well, the one whom you loved is here! Your beloved is back, *Hooray!* This is "gladness." This is delight and "peace," and gratitude. But is it also joy?

Well, and at his appearing, the Son of God has just kept the hardest of all his promises: he rose from the dead, exactly as he said. This is marvelous affirmation, the absolute guarantee that he shall keep to every other promise, from salvation to the sending of the Spirit to the raising of the dead. This is bright, sustaining assurance of faith. Is it also joy?

What causes joy?

What transfigures *you*, you flaming disciple, you burning witness, with such a fusion of joy in the encounter?

This: not just that the Lord was dead, *but that you grieved his death*. That, for three days, you yourself did suffer his absence, and then the whole world was for you a hollow horror. That, despite his promises, this last Sabbath lasted forever and was, to your sorrowing heart, the last of the world after all. You experienced, you actually believed, that the end of Jesus was the end of everything.

Death reigned everywhere.

Death alone.

But in the economy of God, what seems the end is but a preparation. For it is, now, to *that* attitude and into *that* experience that the dear Lord Jesus Christ appears—not only an astonishment, gladness and affirmation, but joy indeed!

It is the experience of genuine grief that prepares for joy.

You see? The disciples approached the Resurrection from their bereavement. For them the death was first, and the death was all. Easter, then, was an explosion of Newness, a marvelous splitting of heaven indeed. But for us, who return backward into the past, the Resurrection comes first, and through *it* we view a death which is, therefore, less consuming, less horrible, even less real. We miss the disciples' terrible, wonderful preparation.

Unless, as now, we attend to the suffering first, to the cross with sincerest pity and vigilant love, to the dying with most faithful care—and thus prepare for joy.

† † †

Jesus, come again!

You need never suffer again. That was done once and for all. But come and remind me of the suffering, so that I recall and regain the purer joy of your rising after all.

Amen.

PART ONE

BETHANY
AND
JERUSALEM

THE FIFTH DAY
MONDAY

MARK 14:1–2

> *It was now two days before the Passover and the feast of Unleavened Bread. And the chief priests and the scribes were seeking how to arrest him by stealth, and kill him; for they said, "Not during the feast, lest there be a tumult of the people."*

The story starts right here. Here, suddenly, Mark locks his Gospel into time.

In one sense, everything heretofore has been preliminary to the crucial event of Jesus' passion. We've learned who Jesus is (but not completely, since he's been coy about his messianic identity and many have erred through the ages in picturing him). We've heard his teachings (but words without action make no story, and his parabolic method of teaching has left many hearing without understanding after all). We've watched his miracles, fine little stories in themselves (but these have grown fewer the closer he's come to Jerusalem, and Jesus himself has diminished their importance by making more of forgiving than of healing paralytics.)

There's more than this, the first thirteen chapters imply: *You ain't seen nothing yet.*

Indeed, if those chapters were all we had from Mark, we'd have a wonder-worker, a charismatic rabbi, a list of ethical lessons, a minor political pest in history—and an enigma. Jesus may have been remarkable, but not essentially different from other notable figures in human memory: no radical revelation of God, no savior of humankind.

The core story starts right here.

Throughout his Gospel until this passage, Mark has been vague about historical time; the time references that join one episode to another have been altogether internal, closed inside the Gospel itself. The events of Jesus' ministry happen "in those days." Which days? Don't know. What time of year? Once or twice we can figure a harvest; besides that, he doesn't say. When things move swiftly, Mark says "immediately." More slowly, they occur "after some days" or "on the same day" or "after six days."

When Jesus journeys from Galilee to Jerusalem, all time references are to that journey: "As he was setting out on his journey, a man . . ."; "they were on the road . . ."; "as he was leaving Jericho . . ."; "and when he drew near Jerusalem . . ." There is the persistent sense of motion in these references. The trip becomes dreadfully significant, foreshadows something momentous at its end, and in this way Mark gives the journey a discrete, nearly serpentine life of its own. But when did it take place? Don't know. What was the rest of the world doing then? Can't tell. What time of year was it? He doesn't say.

There's an odd timeless quality to the appearing and presence of Jesus, and then to his progress toward Jerusalem. Jesus in history is like a dream in waking reality: nearly mythic, strangely untouchable.

But suddenly all that changes.

Look: now it's "two days before the Passover." Suddenly we know precisely the time of year and we can see the rest of the world; we know what the people are doing. Suddenly Jesus is rooted very much in time, terribly touchable, dangerously historical. We grow tense and attentive. A new thing is happening! It's happening within the calendar of human days: Wednesday, the thirteenth day of the month called Nisan. This is no myth, no legend, no mere lesson or instructive biography. This is *the* story Mark intended to tell from the beginning. This is the "something else," revelation, the profounder identity of Jesus: the Savior!

Mark's canny device (of saving till now the link between actual time and his Gospel) wakes us heart and soul to the central event of that Gospel, without which there is no Gospel at all. Listen! Listen! The story is starting right now. . . .

† † †

Jesus:

Forgive me for making much of what's minor in your story, diminishing the important thing. I've demanded miracles, healings, benefits for myself. O Lord, raise the cross as the central beam of my whole life once again!

Amen.

THE SIXTH DAY
TUESDAY

MARK 14:1–2 (again)

> *It was now two days before the Passover and the feast of Unleavened Bread. And the chief priests and the scribes were seeking how to arrest him by stealth, and kill him; for they said, "Not during the feast, lest there be a tumult of the people."*

Here comes Jesus, closer and closer to me. Ah, the closer he comes, the less I like it. His very existence threatens mine. . . .

I've grown used to my way of life. I like the familiarity. I know my place in society, my reputation, my rights and privileges, all of which are comfortable to me. I know what power I have and what responsibilities. I worked hard for these things and deserve to keep them. Behold, I am a person of some prominence—small or large, it doesn't matter: I am! This is me. This is my identity.

But here comes Jesus to Jerusalem, the seat of my existence, the place of my authority—and all of this is threatened. I rule here because Rome allows it and because religious tradition sanctifies it. Rome requires an obedient people. Religion authorizes me to hold them in check. But if the people riot, Rome will strip me of power. If religious practice is undermined, I lose identity. If religion here is ruined, why, the whole world tips in confusion and I slide off the edge.

Yet here comes Jesus, at Passover! At the feast of Unleavened Bread! When Jerusalem's full of pilgrims, swollen five times its size—from 50,000 to 250,000 people! Always the threat of this man is manifested in those whom his presence excites. Look how volatile the people are now! Worse than that, he is questioning religious laws developed over the centuries, the very forms by which we order ourselves and know ourselves and name ourselves.

If order is lost, so am I.

If I lose my power and prominence, I lose my identity, my being, my very self. And then I am *not!*

What then? Why, then I must destroy before I am destroyed. Self-preservation is a law of nature. I will arrest this Jesus by stealth and kill him. Because if I do nothing, I will *be* nothing.

But look: here comes Jesus in my mother, in my spouse, in my children! Always, always he is manifest in those whom he has excited. They seem so fanatical; and their love of Jesus undermines their respect for me and my authority. I'm losing prominence in my own house, and power and honor. Worse, the zealots declare that I should willingly sacrifice these things, though I need them in order to maintain my identity and to be! They say that I should actually welcome the changes Jesus causes here and now—that I should deny my very self!

What then? What will I do to the Jesus in these people, coming closer and closer to the seat of my power, to me?

Well, if I do nothing . . .

† † †

Ah, Jesus,

By the refining fires of your grace reduce my prideful self to ash after all. Let me become a nothing, that you might be the only something for me and in me. Be my all in all, Lord, Master of the Universe!

Amen.

THE SEVENTH DAY
WEDNESDAY

MARK 14:1–9

> It was now two days before the Passover and the feast of
> Unleavened Bread. And the chief priests and the scribes
> were seeking how to arrest him by stealth, and kill him; for
> they said, "Not during the feast, lest there be a tumult of
> the people."
>
> And while he was at Bethany in the house of Simon the
> leper, as he sat at table, a woman came with an alabaster
> flask of ointment of pure nard, very costly, and she broke the
> flask and poured it over his head.
>
> But there were some who said to themselves indignant-
> ly, "Why was the ointment thus wasted? For this ointment
> might have been sold for more than three hundred denarii
> and given to the poor." And they reproached her.
>
> But Jesus said, "Let her alone! Why do you trouble her?
> She has done a beautiful thing to me.
>
> For you always have the poor with you, and whenever
> you will, you can do good to them; but you will not always
> have me. She has done what she could; she has anointed my
> body beforehand for burying. And truly I say to you,
> wherever the gospel is preached in the whole world, what she
> has done will be told in memory of her."

Woman!

What a blessed contrast you make to the rulers in
Jerusalem! They would preserve their power; you come with no

power at all. They vaunt themselves; you have—except for one remarkable characteristic—no self at all.

What is your name that I might address my praise to you? I don't know. Were you someone's mother? I don't know. Were you old, bent by years of experience? Were you a prostitute? Or else praiseworthy for purity and virtue? Were you poor, the ointment an impossible expense for you? Or rich, with easy access to a hundred such flasks? I don't know. Mark never says. I know nothing about you save this: that you anointed the head of my Lord.

Ah, but that's enough to know! That deed alone is your identity, your entire being: your self. It memorializes you forever. "What she has *done*," says Jesus, "will be told in memory of her." Woman, now you are that deed, neither more nor less than that deed. I marvel at you. I pray God that I might do—and therefore be—the same.

For what was your gesture? An act of pure love for Jesus particularly. It was an act so completely focused upon the Christ that not a dram of worldly benefit was gained thereby. Nothing could justify this spillage of some three hundred days' wages, except love alone. The rulers who sought to kill Jesus were motivated by a certain reasonable logic; but your prodigality appears altogether unreasonable—except for reasons of love. The disciples, in fact, were offended by an act that produced nothing, accomplished nothing, fed no poor, served no need. They reproached you as a wastrel.

They were offended by the absurd, an act devoted absolutely to love, to love alone.

But Jesus called it "beautiful."

Who else anointed our High Priest, as priests should surely be anointed in office? Who else anointed our King, the son of David? Who else anointed the body of our Savior for burial? No one but you. I don't know that you consciously recognized these offices of the Lord; but love instinctively sees the truth. Love enhances and names in truth. No one else anointed him and by that gesture declared him *Messiah*, the *Christ*. The act, therefore, was more than beautiful. It was rare and rich with meaning.

And since the act is all there is of you, since humility has reduced you to this single thing alone and now you are no more nor less than your love for the Lord, you yourself are beautiful and rare and rich with meaning.

You *are* the beauty of faithful loving.

To those who do not truly love, you will ever be ephemeral or else an offense, either a shadow or an idiot. To me you are a model. You gave up all; you became nothing at all save love for the Lord; and exactly so you are remembered. Here, "wherever the gospel is preached in the whole world," is love's monument!

You, nameless, anonymous, lovely indeed: thank you.

† † †

Jesus, I love you, I love you!

Cleanse me of anything that is not love for you, even though the world will think me preposterous and my friends—some of whom are your disciples—will not be able to make sense of me. You are all the sense and meaning I need. I love you.

Amen.

THE EIGHTH DAY

THURSDAY

MARK 14:1b, 10–11

> *The chief priests and the scribes were seeking how to arrest him by stealth, and kill him.*
>
> *Then Judas Iscariot, who was one of the twelve, went to the chief priests in order to betray him to them. And when they heard it they were glad, and promised to give him money. And he sought an opportunity to betray him.*

In order to arrest Jesus "by stealth," the rulers need someone like Judas. Enemies must know the habits of their prey—and what better source of such privy knowledge than a friend? Enter Judas Iscariot, a friend who is willing to act like an enemy: a traitor.

The contract that Judas now makes with men of murderous intent is so horrendous that we ask, compulsively, "Why? Why did he do it?" We feel the tale is incomplete without his motive. "Greed!" we figure. Or the more sophisticated among us argue that Judas was moved by a misguided zealotry. In fact, Mark ignores the question of motive altogether. He implies that Judas went voluntarily and (seeing that he accepted the rulers' scheme so easily) with no particular plan of his own in mind. But that is absolutely all Mark cares to say of the mind of Judas.

Perhaps there's a lesson for us in this presentation of the sin apart from its causes, as though motives were merely incidental and ultimately beside the point.

Does the motive of a sin—its rationale, its reasons—make

it any less a sin? Isn't the betrayal of the sovereignty of the Lord in our lives *always* a sin, regardless of the factors that drove us to betray him? Yes! Yet we habitually defend ourselves and diminish our fault by referring to reasons why we "had to" do it. We sinners are so backward that we try to justify ourselves by some condition which preceded the sin. Motives console us. That's why we want so badly to have and to know them.

"Not my fault! He hit me first. I was just protecting myself!"

"Don't blame me! My society was a bad influence on me. My parents set bad examples—abused me, even; never disciplined me. Blame them."

"Hey, man, it's dog-eat-dog. I'm only tryin' to survive."

"I can't help the way I am. Yo!—God made me. God gave me my appetites, right?"

We sinners are so backward! We invert the true source of our justification. It isn't some preliminary cause, some motive *before* the sin that justifies me, but rather the forgiveness of Christ which meets my repentance *after* the sin. If I did it, I'm responsible, whatever the reasons might be. Motives are incidental to the sin *as a sin* and to its expiation. If by excuses I duck my responsibility, I'll never truly repent, and then the forgiveness of Christ will seem incidental to me. (Oh, what a wretched state that would be!) But if I own my responsibility, own *up* to the sin and so repent, then that forgiveness will justify before God even the most horrendous betrayer of Jesus. Even Judas Iscariot. Even me.

Mark's account is right: it needs no motive to be complete. For the betrayer's motive could neither justify nor damn him one whit more. The redeeming love of Jesus alone could have written a happier ending to the tale.

† † †

My dear Jesus:

I wounded my sister today with a word that exalted me more than you because it loved me more than her. I betrayed you, Lord. I destroyed your sovereignty in my life. There is no excuse for the pain I caused for both of you. There is only this:

God, be merciful to me, a sinner!

Amen.

THE NINTH DAY
FRIDAY

MARK 14:12–16

> And on the first day of Unleavened Bread, when they
> sacrificed the Passover lamb, his disciples said to him,
> "Where will you have us go and prepare for you to eat the
> Passover?"
>
> And he sent two of his disciples, and said to them, "Go
> into the city, and a man carrying a jar of water will meet
> you; follow him, and wherever he enters, say to the
> householder, 'The Teacher says, Where is my guest room,
> where I am to eat the Passover with my disciples?' And he
> will show you a large upper room furnished and ready; there
> prepare for us."
>
> And the disciples set out and went to the city, and
> found it as he had told them; and they prepared the
> Passover.

It's Thursday, less than a day before the rulers succeed in
killing Jesus. The machinery of murder is moving through
Jerusalem. Common people, sniffing the winds of rumor with
animal accuracy, cannot be ignorant of the hostilities roused by
this Jesus of Nazareth. The man is a fugitive: to know him is
risky; to be with him, dangerous; but actually to harbor him is
deadly.

Yet he who has had nowhere to lay his head now needs a
house in which to celebrate the Passover.

Who will give me room?

This is forever a measure of the love which Jesus inspires in human hearts: that there was a householder willing to endanger himself by saying, "I will. Come." We know almost as little about this man—and as much—as we know of the woman who anointed Jesus. We know him by his action only; and his deed was love. It was a sacrificial love, which puts itself in harm's way for the sake of the beloved.

"Listen," this householder said in secret to Jesus alone, fully aware of the danger, "we need a signal. I will send a man through the city with a jar of water." (Usually women carried jars, while men bore wineskins; it was a subtle distinction.) "When he sees men following him, he will lead them to my house. No words. No talk. Tell your disciples to identify themselves to me with the words, 'The Teacher says, Where is my guest room?' I'll furnish the upper room with rugs and cushions and a table. Come."

Not all houses had upper rooms; and the few that did had rooms large enough to accommodate a ritual meal for thirteen people. This whispering householder, the "goodman of the house," the head of the family, was not poor. He had something to lose.

Nevertheless, he did not say, "Jesus, I love you with all my heart—but surely you don't expect me to imperil the lives of my wife and my children, do you?"

He did not say, "I love you with all my soul—but let's be practical. How can I love you if I die? And wouldn't you yourself be less than loving to ask such a risk of me?"

He did not say, "I love you with all my mind—but I'm nobody special, no hero of faith. Now, Mother Teresa, maybe, or Martin Luther King might do it. Ask them."

He said, "Come."

Who will give me room? the Lord Jesus asks today.

If we're experienced, we know the risk. The sophisticated world mocks a meek and sheepish Christian. The evil world hates those in whom Christ shines like a light upon its darksome deeds. Even the worldly church will persecute those who, for

Jesus' sake, accuse its compromises, oppose its cold self-righteousness, and so disclose its failure at humble service. It will kill that zeal which threatens its composure.

We know the danger of harboring Christ in a dark world and in a worldly church. They can freeze the one who burns with his bright spirit. They are shamed by a sincerely sacrificial love. They cool their shame by blaming the lover. They cut him from community. They cut him dead.

Yet, *Where is my guest room?* the Teacher asks. And loving him as he loved us, we answer, "Here, Lord. In my heart."

† † †

> Come, Lord Jesus, be my guest,
> and let this room for you be blest.
>
> Amen.

THE TENTH DAY
SATURDAY

MARK 14:17–21

> *And when it was evening he came with the twelve. And as they were at table eating, Jesus said, "Truly, I say to you, one of you will betray me, one who is eating with me."*
>
> *They began to be sorrowful and to say to him one after another, "Is it I?"*
>
> *He said to them, "It is one of the twelve, one who is dipping bread into the dish with me. For the Son of man goes as it is written of him, but woe to that man by whom the Son of man is betrayed! It would have been better for that man if he had not been born."*

"Stop it," says my friend. (Whatever else she may be, sister, spouse, or child, she is by this very cry proving her friendship to me.) "Stop it," she pleads, though I haven't yet done the deed. She sees it coming. She knows its effect. "Stop it. Please! You're hurting me."

Well, and then my tendency is to feel resentment—especially when she's right and I'm wrong. I'm embarrassed by the exposure of my sinfulness.

But the plea, which makes me aware of myself, is no evil. It's a gift. Even if my friend is only protecting herself, this is no less than a gift from God intended to benefit both my friend and myself: her peace, my prudence, my obedience, and finally my peace as well. *Please! You're hurting me.* Oh, let me hear the warning not with anger but with gratitude—and stop.

Judas has no better friend than Jesus.

Loving him, not loathing him, Jesus grants Judas a moment of terrible self-awareness: "One of you will betray me, the one who is dipping bread into the dish with me—"

The deed is not yet done. But Jesus sees it coming and, while yet the sinner contemplates the sin, gives Judas three critical gifts:

1. Knowledge. He knows now the moral quality and the consequence of the deed. This is betrayal. Betrayal is wrong!

2. Free will. Knowledge frees him both from ignorance and from the unconscious compulsion. He now can choose whether to do, or else not to do, the deed.

3. Sole responsibility. If he proceeds with it, then, he alone shall own the deed.

What more can a friend do than Jesus has done—especially in the present context? This is the Passover meal, after all. Judas would therefore be "lifting his heel" against an intimate, one who shares custom and kinship and immediate trust with him.

Moreover, they have just drunk the second cup of wine and recounted the story of Israel's salvation; Jesus, as head of the house, is dipping bread in bitter herbs and stewed fruit. The gesture and the dish are traditional signs of Israel's suffering. But right now they also symbolize the horror of Judas's sin. If he does not stop, *he* shall become the cause of bitter suffering! *He* shall be to Jesus what Egypt was to Israel. His act shall offend the very salvation God prepared for his beloved. It will outrage heaven.

Jesus shall surely "go as it was written of him." But now Judas can't help but see the true treachery of his sin and might choose *not* to be the one by whom Jesus is betrayed. He might choose the quicker, lesser pain: with the others to "be sorrowful" and, louder than the others, to confess, "Yes, it is I." He might admit the love in the gifts that Jesus gives him:

Stop it! Stop it, please! You're hurting me.

The cry of my friend feels harsh. Perhaps I'll hear the

accusation only and harden myself in my sin and, angrier still, continue.

Or maybe I will realize the love of God in her plea and suffer my conscience to hurt and confess myself a sinner and repent and stop. And stop. And—given three gifts by the grace of the dear Lord—stop!

† † †

Holy Jesus,

Send your angels always, always to warn me of my sinning. And grant me, please, the true humility to heed them. I yearn to grow more and more like you!

Amen.

THE ELEVENTH DAY

MONDAY

MARK 14:22–25

> And as they were eating, he took bread and blessed and broke
> it and gave it to them and said, "Take; this is my body."
> And he took the cup, and when he had given thanks he gave
> it to them, and they all drank of it. And he said to them,
> "This is my blood of the covenant, which is poured out for
> many. Truly, I say to you, I shall not drink again of the
> fruit of the vine until that day when I drink it new in the
> kingdom of God."

*T*he Lord Jesus, the same night in which he was betrayed—

When is a mother more inclined to cuddle her children?
When they're a nasty, insolent brood, disobedient and disrespectful of her motherhood? Or when they are cuddly?

When will a father likelier give good gifts to his children?
When they've just ruined the previous gift, by negligence or by downright wickedness? When they are sullen and self-absorbed?
Or when they manifest genuine goodness and self-responsibility?

But the love of Jesus is utterly unaccountable—except that
he is God and God is love. It has no cause in us. It reacts to, or repays, or rewards just nothing in us. It is beyond human measure, beyond human comprehension. It takes my breath away.

For when did Jesus choose to give us the supernal,
enduring gift of his presence, his cuddling, his dear communing with us? When we were worthy of the gift, good people indeed?

Hardly. It was precisely when we were most unworthy. When our wickedness was directed particularly at him.

Listen, children: it was to the insolent and the hateful that he gave his gift of personal love.

"As they were eating, he took bread and blessed and broke it and gave it to them and said—"

With the apostle Paul the pastor repeats: *The Lord Jesus, the same night in which he was betrayed, took bread.* Oh, let that pastor murmur those words, *the same night,* with awe. For who among us can hear them just before receiving the gift of Christ's intimacy and not be overcome with wonder, stunned at such astonishing love? The context qualifies that love. The time defines it. And ever and ever again, these words remind us of the times: *The same night in which he was betrayed—*

"While we were still weak," says Paul, "at the right time Christ died for the ungodly." Not for the godly and the good, but "while we were yet sinners Christ died for us." Then! That same night! When absolutely nothing recommended us. When "we were enemies." Enemies! In the night when his people betrayed him—the night of intensest enmity—the dear Lord Jesus said, "This is my blood of the covenant, poured out for many." Then! Can we comprehend the joining of two such extremes, the good and the evil together? In the night of gravest human treachery he gave the gift of himself. And the giving has never ceased. The holy communion continues today.

But in that *same* night he remembered our need. In that *same* night he provided the sacrament which would forever contain his grace and touch his comfort into us.

Oh, this is a love past human expectation. This is beyond all human deserving. This, therefore, is a love so celestial that it shall endure long and longer than we do.

This is grace.

† † †

Behold, Lord, I am of small account:

What shall I say to thee? I lay my hand upon my mouth. Your love is too wonderful for me; it is high; I can't understand it. But this I do: I dwell within it, silently, gratefully, faithfully, believing in it after all.

Amen.

PART TWO

GETHSEMANE

THE TWELFTH DAY
TUESDAY

❧

MARK 14:26–31

And when they had sung a hymn, they went out to the Mount of Olives.

And Jesus said to them, "You will all fall away; for it is written, 'I will strike the shepherd, and the sheep will be scattered.' But after I am raised up, I will go before you to Galilee."

Peter said to him, "Even though they all fall away, I will not."

And Jesus said to him, "Truly, I say to you, this very night, before the cock crows twice, you will deny me three times."

But he said vehemently, "If I must die with you, I will not deny you."

And they all said the same.

Hey, look me over, Lord! Check me out! I know I wasn't worth much before—but I've changed, right? I'm your solid citizen now, a solid Christian, loving you and trusting you, forgiving my neighbor as I would be forgiven. Why, I've confessed your name at work, and you know how grim those guys can be. But they know I'm a Christian. They don't curse near *me* no more. Feel my muscle! Bigger, right? I'm your man! Hey, I'm your disciple!

(So says the self-satisfied Christian.

(No one can see in the night, but he's wearing a beatific

expression and strutting rather like a rooster. There are eleven others strung out and strolling down the dark road. This one has taken the lead beside a smaller man whose whole manner is slow and broken by sorrow. The smaller man says—)

You will all fall away.

Whoa! You can't mean that! Not *all* of us. Not me! I mean, okay: I know folks who could care less about you, right? Skip church, don't pray but when there's trouble, love their cars more than you. They say they're Christian, but when it comes to the crunch they drop you, Jesus. I pray. I do—daily and long, because I love you! I go to church. I serve on seven boards. I tithe, I fast (though no one knows but you)—I mean, I really *practice* my faith! I visit people in the county jail, right? Look, even though everyone else falls away, I won't!

(The small man halts, forcing the strong one to stop and be still. To him sadly, to him particularly, the small man says—)

Truly, this very night before the cock crows twice, you will deny me three times.

No! No, you don't know me! Oh, Jesus, how can you doubt me like that? Me, of all people! Me, who loves you the most! Don't I always speak up for you? Okay, okay—what should I do to prove my love? Tell me! You want me to quit my job? Sell everything? Become a missionary? I mean it! You want me to *die* for you? I will, Lord. I promise, I will. But I'll never, never deny you!

(The smaller man turns and continues to walk through the night, silently. He does not answer the vehemence of the strong disciple. He will let actions speak for themselves.

(For he knows the strong man very well.

(And better than any, he understands the relationship of faith: that if anyone continues in loving relationship with him, it is *his* love that preserves it, not the love of the other, nor all the piety, nor all the goodness a Christian can muster.

(The big disciple, truly wounded by his Lord's mistrust, keeps muttering—)

I love you, Jesus. I really do love you—

(And he does—as many Christians do! But great love risks a greater pride. For the very strength of their loving sometimes dazzles and flatters them—until they trust that love more than its Lord. But their loving response to Jesus, however strong, is always exactly that: a response to Jesus, empowered by Jesus. *He* enables the loving!

(And even now, near the Mount of Olives, his sad eyes say—)

Peter, Peter, Christian! Soon, in pain, you will discover that it's not your love, not your goodness or knowledge or prayer, no, not all your strength that keeps us together. I do that. I alone, your Lord, do that.

† † †

Jesus,

Make me meek, that I may be strong in you.

Amen.

THE THIRTEENTH DAY
WEDNESDAY

MARK 14:32–42

And they went to a place which was called Gethsemane; and he said to his disciples, "Sit here while I pray."

And he took with him Peter and James and John, and began to be greatly distressed and troubled. And he said to them, "My soul is very sorrowful, even to death. Remain here, and watch."

And going a little farther, he fell on the ground and prayed that, if it were possible, the hour might pass from him. And he said, "Abba, Father, all things are possible to thee. Remove this cup from me; yet not what I will, but what thou wilt."

And he came and found them sleeping, and he said to Peter, "Simon, are you asleep? Could you not watch one hour? Watch, and pray that you may not enter into temptation; the spirit indeed is willing, but the flesh is weak."

And again he went away and prayed, saying the same words. And again he came and found them sleeping, for their eyes were very heavy; and they did not know what to answer him.

And he came a third time and said to them, "Are you still sleeping and taking your rest? It is enough; the hour has come; the Son of man is betrayed into the hands of sinners. Rise. Let us be going. See, my betrayer is at hand."

Night. There is a cold light falling from the indifferent stars—a light like the finest of snows, pale on the ground, pale on the hair and shoulders of a sad band of men moving outside the city.

They pause by a grove of black trees. Four men separate themselves and enter the trees.

Listen! One man is groaning. His breath comes in quick pants, compulsively. Listen: "Oh. Oh. Oh, God. Oh." He goes alone, now, deeper among the trees—while the other three arrange themselves on the ground, their backs against the treetrunks. These three begin to nod. Soon, they sleep.

The woods are pale and silent.

That one man, totally alone, is swaying back and forth as if dizzy, his face in his hands. Suddenly he crumples to the ground. "Abba! Abba!" The sound is strangled in his throat. His fingers dig dirt like the roots of the trees. His chin and his beard grind against the earth.

"Abba, Father, I don't want to do this. Please! You can do anything; then take this cup away from me—"

The man's voice is hoarse, a kind of guttural barking. But then he sucks air and howls at the top of his lungs, "Hell is in that cup! Death and damnation are in that cup! My Father, my Father, it will tear me away from you! No, I don't want to do this! No! Sin is in that cup—and if I drink it you won't look at me, you will loathe me, I will hate myself! I don't want to drink it! Abba, Abba, take the cup away from me—"

The man twists his body underneath the trees, then holds himself in a tense, unnatural posture, his face upward, his eyes shut, his breathing sharp through his teeth. He grimaces, as if smiling, then whispers almost inaudibly, whispers as soft as the leaves: "Nevertheless . . . not what I want . . . what you want . . . do."

When, in the pale starlight, this man returns to the three he left behind, he finds them slumped and snoring. He is alone. Even beside his friends he is completely alone.

And so he prays a second time as though he had not prayed the first. He prays till the sweat runs down his temples. His voice is a wolf's howl in the woods, "Abba!"—and still his friends are slumbering.

His third prayer is so quiet and so private an anguish that his body does not move. He waits in darkness, in a perfect silence for an answer.

And when he returns to his friends the final time, waking them with the news of his own betrayal—"Rise, let us be going"—this, in that hour, is what the solitary man is doing: drinking. Drinking.

† † †

My death, O Lord!
My sin, my hell, and my damnation were in that cup.
My gratitude is unspeakable.
My wonder is silence.
My life is yours.

Amen.

THE FOURTEENTH DAY
THURSDAY

MARK 14:35–36

> And going a little farther, he fell on the ground and prayed
> that, if it were possible, the hour might pass from him. And
> he said, "Abba, Father, all things are possible to thee;
> remove this cup from me; yet not what I will, but what thou
> wilt."

"Lord," the disciples had asked in an earlier, easier time,
"teach us to pray." And Jesus had answered by teaching them
certain words: "When you pray," he said, "say . . ."

The prayer he spoke then we call *The Lord's*.

But Jesus teaches the same thing twice. And the second
lesson is not words only; deeds make up the prayer as well,
and passion and experience—the whole person dramatically
involved.

Words alone might be as hollow and irrelevant as ping-
pong balls. But now the Lord reveals how prayer can be the
expression of an event already in progress; it is human experience finding its voice—and by that voice directing itself wholly
(the whole experience, action, emotion, thought, desire, body,
and spirit) straight to God.

Behold: what takes place in the Garden of Gethsemane is
the Lord's Prayer actually *happening*, as though the earlier
words were a script and this is the drama itself:

—Jesus cries his deepest and desperate desire: that the
hour, by the power of his Father, pass away from him. This is

the living substance of the sixth petition: *Save us from the time of trial.*

—Jesus pleads three times, "Remove this cup from me," the plea of the seventh petition: *Deliver us from evil.*

—But under every request of his own, he places an attitude of faithful obedience to his Father, saying, "Yet not what I will, but what thou wilt." Here is the third petition, which prepares us properly for any answer God may give all other petitions: *Thy will be done on earth as it is in heaven.*

—Implicit, hereafter, in his entering into "the hour" of trial after all is his personal conviction that "the time is fulfilled, and the kingdom of God is at hand." Jesus, now more than ever in his ministry, is the living embodiment of the second petition, *Thy kingdom come.* Right now, his acceptance of the Father's will *is* the coming of that kingdom here!

—And he begins both prayers the same. But whereas the first might have seemed a formal address to "Our Father," this latter cry is a howl, a spontaneous, needful plea: "Abba, Father!" Here is a child who cannot survive apart from this relationship. By crying "Abba!" he hurls himself at the holy parent: he runs like a child; like a child he begs attention; but also like a perfect child he trusts his daddy to do right and well.

When Jesus teaches us to pray, he does not teach plain recitation. Rather, he calls us to a way of being. He makes of prayer a doing. And by his own extreme example, he shows that prayer is the active relationship between ourselves, dear little children, and the dear Father, *Abba.*

Who can pray The Lord's Prayer now with words and not with the heart's experience?

† † †

Abba!
Dear Father in heaven,
Whose name is so holy!
Bring your kingdom here;
Let your will be done on earth as it is in heaven;

Give us today our daily bread;
Forgive us our sins as we forgive those who sin against us;
Save us from tests of our righteousness;
Deliver us from every evil.
Yours is the kingdom, the power and glory, forever!

Amen, amen.

THE FIFTEENTH DAY
FRIDAY

MARK 14:43–49

> And immediately, while he was still speaking, Judas came,
> one of the twelve, and with him a crowd with swords and
> clubs, from the chief priests and the scribes and the elders.
>
> Now the betrayer had given them a sign, saying, "The
> one I shall kiss is the man; seize him and lead him away
> under guard."
>
> And when he came, he went up to him at once and
> said, "Master!"
>
> And he kissed him.
>
> And they laid hands on him and seized him. But one of
> those who stood by drew his sword and struck the slave of the
> high priest and cut off his ear.
>
> And Jesus said to them, "Have you come out as against
> a robber, with swords and clubs to capture me? Day after day
> I was with you in the temple teaching, and you did not seize
> me. But let the scriptures be fulfilled."

There comes an orange snake eastward through the night. A
snake of fire, a long snake of torches. Perhaps the disciples
glance down from the Mount of Olives and see it and do not
understand. Jesus understands. It winds the same path they
themselves have followed from the city. It winks through the
trees in a smooth and silent, serpentine approach. It is a fatal
snake. It kills by kissing.

The binding strength of that snake is the armed guard of

the Temple and the police of the Sanhedrin. Behold how the servants of God can bite!

But the head of the snake is one of the twelve, a disciple of Jesus. Behold how an intimate may kiss for other reasons than affection and respect.

Suddenly Judas Iscariot appears beside the group of friends who stand outside the Garden of Gethsemane. Smiling. Judas is smiling. And claiming his accustomed place. And holding his torch aloft to shed light on the faces around him. Peering into these faces. Looking for . . . no, not for John, not James; no, not for Andrew or for Peter, though he greets them all with familiar nods. He's looking for . . . ah!

The snake coils now into a thick knot of bodies and flame before the disciples. It has scores of eyes all flashing red in torchlight. Its scales are weapons, swords and clubs adown its sides. Its silence is tense, dead menace in close proximity—and it stinks of human sweat.

The disciples swallow, nervous and uncertain.

Jesus gazes and waits.

Now, the serpent was more subtle than any beast of the field which the Lord God made. From the beginning its movement was smooth, its manner mild, its promise to elevate whom it would eat. It was a murderer even from the beginning, a liar, the father of lies, and the father, so Jesus once declared, of—

The serpent strikes!

Smiling, Judas says, "Rabbi!" and kisses Jesus. A sign of devotion. A sign, for the Temple guard, that this is the one to seize and lead away. A lie.

In a garden once the Lord God decreed enmity between the serpent and the seed of the woman, enmity to the death. In a garden again that enmity produces this pathetic assault: a kiss that can kill.

But the serpent, that father of lies, is father too of what other brood? Why, of a human brood!—of those who know the nature of God and yet reject him! "You," said Jesus once, "you are of your father the devil, and your will is to do your father's desires!" (But read all of John 8:34–47!)

Even so do children, tragically, exchange one Father for another. How long must it be before the second father's exposed as a fraud and a murderer?

And even so, with the meekest of gestures, has the war for the world been engaged. With a kiss. And the kiss has a tooth. And the snake that struck the Lord has a back of fire and a body of human opinion.

† † †

O Jesus,

This is such a sad meditation; yet this is just the start of "the hour," first sips from the cup of your suffering!

Send even now your Spirit of Comfort, the Paraclete, since it is in your grace alone that I can bear to hear the horrible word and to see this story to conclusion. Please!

Amen.

THE SIXTEENTH DAY
SATURDAY

MARK 14:50–52

> And they all forsook him and fled.
>
> And a young man followed him with nothing but a linen cloth about his body; and they seized him, but he left the linen cloth and ran away naked.

Here, suddenly, appears "a young man" whose entire person shall be reduced in history to this single act: that he also suddenly disappeared—in fear and forever.

Things are heating up. In the fires of serious persecution the truer elements of one's character now are revealed. Everything fraudulent, cheap, or hypocritical burns. Every pretense turns to ash. All my false words blow away. What I really am—the core character, the thing God sees when he looks at me, the irreducible person—I am indeed before the people. What I am, I am: I seem no more nor less than the thing I am. No clothing hides me—no, not so much as a linen cloth.

Ecce homo! Behold the thing itself, unaccommodated man, poor and bare and forked and—what? What is the stuff of the *me?*

What? Well, there was the woman who anointed Jesus for his burial. That nameless "she," when reduced to the basic character, was love, pure love, love lavish and sweeter than nard, but love alone: this was the *she.*

But again what, in the extremes of human persecution and pain, is the actual *me* of myself? Well, here appears this fellow who "followed him" only until his person is seized. And then, spontaneously, the young man takes to his heels and flees—to save his *self*, which, therefore, is the core of him and the truth of his character. Where the woman was love at the core, this nameless "he" has a *self* which he will not lose, nor give up, nor deny, but which at all costs he will save. This is the *he*: his self alone.

And who, under the same circumstances, am I? Or what shall I prove to be?

It's not as if I haven't been warned. Jesus has spoken at least three times of his suffering and death—and fully as many times he's declared that if I intend to come after him I must deny my *self* and take my cross and follow him. "For those," he said, "who would save their lives will lose them, and those who lose their lives for my sake and the gospel's will save them." Who can forget such words? "Go, sell what you have; and come, follow me." Those words. And these: "The cup that I drink—you will drink."

The cup.

And I, with all his disciples, heard and agreed. "Yes," we said, "we are able to drink that cup." And I meant it! No, I was not lying. I would do anything for Jesus. But that was during the period of words and learning. A sort of prelude, I suppose. Sunday school, confirmation, sermons, study: preparation. A time of pieties and promises.

Well—here comes the cup!

Here's the real world, and the world's at war! And my deeds are my words now, and deeds don't lie.

O Jesus, they're grabbing at me! *Me!* Suddenly I'm not an observer. I'm involved! They're tearing off my last possession! What am I going to do? Sell out? Sell everything to save my life, my bare *self*? Run away naked?

Or what'll I do? Lord, you don't seem a very strong force beside me now; you're suffering too! And you want me to *stay* with you? Do you know how much your call to "deny myself" looks exactly like dying right now? I mean really *dying*?

What will I do? And when I do—
—what will I be?
And who—?

† † †

Christ!

Take my life: I consecrate it to thee. Take all that I have
and all that I am; replace the *self* in me with thine own holy
self—that when the wicked world would kill me it finds me
already drowned in thee, untouchable. Death in the world
is death indeed. But death in thee is life forever!

Amen!

PART THREE

THE
HIGH PRIEST'S
HOUSE

THE SEVENTEENTH DAY
MONDAY

MARK 14:53–65

> And they led Jesus to the high priest; and all the chief
> priests and the elders and the scribes were assembled. And
> Peter had followed him at a distance, right into the
> courtyard of the high priest, where he was sitting with the
> guards and warming himself at the fire.
>
> Now the chief priests and the whole council sought
> testimony against Jesus to put him to death; but they found
> none. For many bore false witness against him, and their
> witness did not agree.
>
> Some stood up and bore false witness against him,
> saying, "We heard him say, 'I will destroy this temple that is
> made with hands, and in three days I will build another,
> not made with hands.'" Yet not even so did their testimony
> agree.
>
> And the high priest stood up in the midst and asked
> Jesus, "Have you no answer to make? What is it that these
> men testify against you?"
>
> But he was silent and made no answer.
>
> Again the high priest asked him, "Are you the Christ,
> the Son of the Blessed?"
>
> And Jesus said, "I am. You will see the Son of man
> seated at the right hand of Power, coming with the clouds of
> heaven."
>
> And the high priest tore his garments and said, "Why
> do we still need witnesses? You have heard his blasphemy.
> What is your decision?"

And they all condemned him as deserving death.
And some began to spit on him and to cover his face
and to strike him, saying to him, "Prophesy!"
And the guards received him with blows.

The city has not yet awakened. The night is starless now, and cold. Jesus, surrounded by a tired guard, walks back through Jerusalem's streets. No one says anything. Jesus' eyes are steadfastly forward, his mouth closed.

He is led through the courtyard of the high priest's house. People glance up from firelight as he passes. He ascends the steps to an upper room, saying nothing.

This room is lit by yellow flame and oil-light. It's crowded. All round its walls men stand and stare. The air stinks of hasty waking. No one is carefully dressed. No one cares. They number enough to make a quorum; that's what matters: their vote will represent the whole Sanhedrin.

Jesus is led to the center, facing a table. He stands straight and solitary, saying nothing.

Caiaphas—politic, smooth, long-tenured and shrewd: High Priest Caiaphas sits at the table, presiding. He nods. Jesus does not. Caiaphas is robed in a rich red. Jesus is roped.

The trial begins.

One by one men move from the walls, formally to testify against the prisoner. But as one by one they return to their places, it becomes apparent that they are annoying the high priest. His eyelids droop with contempt. Their stories contradict each other. Their evidence is inadmissible.

Caiaphas knows the verdict he wants. Everyone knows. So why can't two idiots agree on a single story?

His anger shows in the white of his lips, in his furious silence. Men flick glances toward one another. The air crackles with fear. Jesus gazes straight at Caiaphas, waiting.

"I . . . he," says a fellow, creeping forward, "I heard him say he'd destroy the temple—"

78

"When?" asks the high priest.

"Well, something about three days—"

"When did he threaten to destroy the temple?"

"Oh! Well, maybe three days ago?"

"No, no, no!" says another man, trying to be helpful. "I heard that at least three years ago—"

BOOM! The high priest strikes the table, dismisses these fools, rises, and takes the floor himself.

To Jesus he hisses, "Have you nothing to say in your own defense?"

But Jesus continues to gaze at Caiaphas, steadfastly still and silent.

"What? What? What?" the high priest sneers, his voice an oil of irony: "Are you the Messiah, then?"

Nervous giggles flee through the room.

But now the prisoner speaks, and what he says stops laughter altogether: "I am."

For an instant the high priest freezes. Everyone freezes. Then, both horror and hilarity in his small eye, Caiaphas explodes.

"Blasphemy!" he roars. He takes his robe in two hands and tears it and shows the pieces to the council. "Blasphemy, blasphemy!" he sings. "So what is your verdict?"

The council is beaming. The room is relieved. The thing will end well after all.

"Death!" says the council. "Of course."

So heartened are folks by this turn of events, so sure of the prisoner's folly and of their own superiority, that quite fearlessly they spit on him. And he takes it! Well, then they cudgel their brains to think up rather more complex games of scorn. They blindfold him and hit him and ask him, like some folk-tale Messiah, to prophesy: "Figure it out. Who hit you?"

Jesus looks out the window. The sky is streaked with grey. Morning is coming. He says nothing now. He says nothing at all.

† † †

Jesus, I follow you.

Whenever discipleship puts me in peril, give me the gift of a holy silence—to speak the truth, no less, no more.

Amen.

THE EIGHTEENTH DAY

TUESDAY

MARK 14:61–62

> He was silent and made no answer. Again the high priest asked him, "Are you the Christ, the Son of the Blessed?"
>
> And Jesus said, "I am; and you will see the Son of man seated at the right hand of Power and coming with the clouds of heaven."

Oh, what a message comes in the timing here! And what a caution to Christians who want a hero for their Christ!

Only now, finally, does Jesus publicly claim the office of Messiah. Now! Why, any fool could choose a better time than this, right? Wrong! Anyone who did would be a fool indeed, for he would pervert the character and the intention of the Christ.

Now is the best time. Now *is* the Christ's time, because this *is* the Christ: a prisoner and a failure.

From the beginning of his ministry, Jesus charged those who experienced his power to say nothing about it. Wonders and miracles, evidently, were not the central purpose of his coming. They may have been signs pointing *to* the Messiah; but they were not the definition of the messianic office.

And when he was at the height of his ministry (as the world assesses height, as the world assesses greatness) he demanded that no one say he was the "Christ." When he was dazzling crowds, confuting enemies, causing shepherds and lepers and kings to ask, "Who *is* this man?"; when masses were "astonished beyond measure, saying, 'He has done all things well, the deaf to hear, the dumb to speak!'"; even when Simon Peter explicitly confessed, "You are the Christ"—Jesus commanded them "to tell no one about him." Apparently none of this was the real work of the "Christ."

Even when Peter, James, and John saw his celestial glory in the transfiguration—saw Jesus revealed as the fulfillment of the whole Old Testament—he told them to shut up.

The world would have misunderstood the glory.

The world might have expected a warrior-king, someone triumphant in its own terms. A winner, you know. A number-one, against-all-odds, pride-inspiring, tear-in-my-eye, flat-out, all-round, good-guy *winner!* A hero.

Only when that characterization is rendered absurd and impossible does Jesus finally accept the title "Christ."

Christian, come and look closely: it is when Jesus is humiliated, most seeming weak, bound and despised and alone and defeated that he finally answers the question, "Are you the Christ?"

Now, for the record, yes: *I am.*

It is only in incontrovertible powerlessness that he finally links himself with power: "And you will see the Son of man seated at the right hand of power." Because any display of messianic power is far, far in the future—in his and in ours together, on the last day. *The last day of the world, not today!*

This, then, is the Christ that Jesus would have us know and accept and (O Christian!) reflect:

One who came to die.

One who, in the assessment of this age, failed—an embarrassment, a folly, a stumbling block. An offense!

One crucified.

Here in the world, the Christ and his followers hang ever on a cross. The cross is foremost, because a faithless world cannot see past it to the Resurrection.

And even for the faithful the cross must always be first, because the Resurrection is only as real (both in history and in our hearts) as the death is real.

What then of our big churches, Christian? What of our bigger parking lots, our rich coffers, our present power to change laws in the land, our political clout, our glory for Christ, our triumphant and thundering glory for Christ? It is excluded! All of it. It befits no Christian, for it was rejected by Jesus.

If ever we persuade the world (or ourselves) that we have a hero in our Christ, then we have lied. Or else we are deceived, having accepted the standards of this world.

He came to die *beneath* the world's iniquity. The world, therefore, can only look *down* on him whom it defeated—down in hatred until it repents; but then it is the world no more.

Likewise, the world will look down on us—down in contempt until it elevates the Christ it sees in us; but then it won't be our enemy any more, will it?

† † †

Christ Crucified—

When I was offended by you—by the miserable figure you cut in this world and by the humiliation you require of me—then I was offended by the cross. It had become a scandal to me, a stumbling-block; and I was conformed to the world.

Forgive me! Let your forgiveness transform me, so that I am like you, and that I *like* to be like you!

Amen.

THE NINETEENTH DAY
WEDNESDAY

MARK 14:65

> And some began to spit on him and to cover his face and to strike him, saying to him, "Prophesy!" And the guards received him with blows.

JOHN 3:19–20

> And this is the judgment, that the light has come into the world, and men loved darkness rather than light, because their deeds were evil. For every one who does evil hates the light, and does not come to the light, lest his deeds should be exposed.

Be careful. We humans tend to dehumanize our enemies. We drop them to a species lower than our own, thinking ourselves more highly developed, more complex, intelligent, virtuous, sensitive, etc. They, in our judgment, are beasts—animals in thought and habit and desire.

And since those who spit on Jesus are enemies of ours (since we love Jesus), we accept Mark's description of their brutish behavior. It's pretty juvenile stuff, don't you think? Spitting and hitting? Almost comic-book for nastiness. Yet we don't question it, because it fits our picture of the foes of Jesus (people different from us; people decidedly worse than us—retarded in morals, retarded in mind). Pigs grunt. Geese honk. Our enemies stink and spit.

Be careful. They may be the enemies of our Lord at the moment when he is arraigned. But they are not different from us. They're quite as complex as we are now—and we have been what they are, enemies of Jesus. If we diminish them, we diminish ourselves.

Listen: sometimes the smile of a genuinely good man infuriates you. You hate the smile specifically—because it reveals a difference! Because the kindness in him is shining on some unkindness in you. Get it? You hate that sort of light. You want to slap the smile right off his face, right? And if he gives signs of forgiving you, why, then his moral superiority becomes simply insufferable. If he's *that* good, think how bad it makes you out to be! Well of course he can't be *that* good. So he's a hypocrite—and you're right to get rid of him, by gestures of perfect contempt, if not by death.

Get it? We spit on him not because we're beasts but because he's not *worth* spit. It's a very complex thing after all.

True goodness accuses true evil; the better the good one, the worse the bad one, and the more outraged for being shown so.

To sinners, the mere presence of goodness can feel like an attack. It triggers guilt. Guilt hurts. Guilt forces us to notice ourselves, thereby to question and to second-guess ourselves; and such an internal process destroys the joy of an unconscious life. We are altogether *too* conscious, suddenly—too self-aware. Doubt destroys the thoughtless satisfactions.

So: who provoked such complications and pain? Him we hate!

Goodness is a spotlight. It shines on our shame, our filth, our deformities; it picks out the parts we hide from the world and even from ourselves. We will strike at that light. We'll haul it into court, discredit it, and smash it in order to put it out. We'll spit on it and belittle it. We'll blindfold it, hit it, and ask it to prophesy—all to prove what a fraud this "prophet" is! (And to dehumanize him! Get it?)

Where patience shines, impatience is revealed and hates the attention. Kindness shows unkindness to be hideous. True joy

85

intensifies true bitterness; gentleness enrages belligerence; and self-control proves the pig to be nothing but a pig.

The real trial in Caiaphas's house is not of the guilt of Jesus. Rather, Jesus is judging the guilt of the others, not by speaking, but by being perfectly innocent. Innocence accuses its accusers. (This is the great war between secular powers and genuine religion; the trial continues even today.) They hate it. They scream to drown the sweeter truth; they condemn him to death in order to put out the light. They want dearly to put out the light.

† † †

Save me, Lord, from blaming anyone but myself:
    —not you (whose innocence spotlights my sin),
    —not your foes (whose sins are my own),
    —not people whose virtues reveal my evil.

    I must suffer my guilt, my own guilt; this is the pain of an earnest repentance; and repentance alone can hear your forgiveness. I beg your forgiveness.

Amen.

THE TWENTIETH DAY
THURSDAY

MARK 14:66–72

> And as Peter was below in the courtyard, one of the maids of the high priest came; and seeing Peter warming himself, she looked at him and said, "You also were with the Nazarene, Jesus."
>
> But he denied it, saying, "I neither know nor understand what you mean." And he went out into the gateway.
>
> And the maid saw him and began again to say to the bystanders, "This man is one of them."
>
> But again he denied it.
>
> And after a little while again the bystanders said to Peter, "Certainly you are one of them; for you are a Galilean."
>
> But he began to invoke a curse on himself and to swear, "I do not know this man of whom you speak."
>
> And immediately the cock crowed a second time.
>
> And Peter remembered how Jesus had said, "Before the cock crows twice, you will deny me three times."
>
> And he broke down and wept.

There's a war inside the strong disciple. (The stronger the disciple, the worse the war!) There's a struggle in Peter between good and evil, between these two commitments: to his Lord and to his own survival.

The man is here, after all. Whether boldly or secretly, he has entered the den of the enemy. He's allowed himself to be enclosed in the high priest's courtyard. Love is stronger than fear right now. Maybe the nap in Gethsemane—especially after his bully boast never to leave the Lord—shamed him into some sort of action. He's here, staring into the fire.

What can he do for Jesus? Can't raise an army. Can't even draw his own sword any more. Pray, maybe. Support the Lord by his presence. Be here. Being here's a witness, isn't it? *Yes, if it becomes known.* Well, even if it isn't known, it takes courage just to be here, hunched by an alien fire, the flames on his face.

He's trying to decipher the voices behind him, the murmuring in the upper room: how is it going for Jesus—?

But suddenly a woman is talking to him. "You were with the Nazarene!" And suddenly he's frightfully aware of himself, his immediate situation.

"No," he says, not looking up. A spontaneous deflection of attention. He wishes people wouldn't notice him. A spontaneous defection, were the truth known.

"No," he says to her searching gaze, "I don't even know what you're talking about."

She does not stop staring at him.

So he gets up and walks to the gateway. He is exceedingly aware of himself right now. Of his *self.* He has lied to save that self. On the other hand, despite the staring, he has not actually left the place. Even when the woman tells others of her suspicions, he stays. Her voice carries to the gateway; the eyes of the others are turning in his direction; he tries to deflect the public awareness by a small shrug, a chuckle at the woman's error, and a second denial: "I don't know that man, heh-heh."

The war must be horrible now: part of him is desperate to save himself; a second denial can't be involuntary; he has sundered his fortunes from those of his Lord.

Nevertheless, that he should make a second denial at all proves he still intends to stay. Even now, in the midst of explicit danger, his cover blown, his presence, then, a witness after all, Simon Peter sweats it out and loves the Lord and does not leave.

Right *now*—after the second denial, before the third—the

forces warring in Peter's soul seem terribly equal: a tremendous, selfless love for Jesus keeps him there, while a consuming self-interest keeps him lying. He denies himself to stay by his Lord. He denies his Lord to save himself. Both. Good and bad.

Peter is paralyzed between the good that he would and the evil that he is.

I see this. I recognize this. I cannot divorce myself from this—for Peter's moral immobilization is mine as well! I am in the courtyard with him, watching. I, too, am good and evil in terribly equal parts—and helpless.

Two things alone can break the impasse for Peter and me.

1. The dreadful, merciful word of the Lord, which calls a sin a *sin* and mine: my fault, my own most grievous killing of Christ in my life to keep that life my *own*.

When Peter's denial reaches such extremes that he draws down death in "a curse on himself" (the logical end of all our sinning!) Jesus intervenes: "And immediately the cock crowed a second time, and Peter remembered" what Jesus had said. Peter may have left Jesus; but Jesus—by wonderful means of remembering him, rooster's crows like sacraments—has not left Peter.

2. Our sorrow when we see the sin, our personal repentance.

Rather than striking back at the Lord, spitting on him, blindfolding and despising him, we rush out to a private darkness, Peter and I. In the alleys, in the shadows of Friday's dawning, we break down and burst into tears.

† † †

O Lord Jesus:
> It is no small thing that the very first word of your resurrection carried a message for Peter: "Tell his disciples *and Peter* that he is going before you to Galilee." In the naming of the man you forgave him; you received him again, an apostle, pure and strong and loving and beloved.
>> Well, I too have wept for my sinful denials of you. Christ, I beg the same forgiveness!
>>> Amen.

PART FOUR

THE
PRAETORIUM

THE TWENTY-FIRST DAY
FRIDAY

MARK 15:1

> *And as soon as it was morning, the chief priests with the elders and scribes and the whole council held a consultation; and they bound Jesus and led him away and delivered him to Pilate.*

Oh, my Lord, the dawn of your deathday!

The sky is grey, the roofs of Jerusalem dark in the grey, and the street at your feet is dim.

You walk from the high priest's house to the Praetorium. Are you tired? Have you slept at all?

You ate last night—but that was last night. You prayed last night an exhausted prayer. And last night you endured a long, malign investigation—you alone, and none beside you to support you. You suffered conventional gestures of contempt and official rejection: the death sentence, accompanied by degrading games. Did they wash your face of their spittle? No. It sticks to you still. To them you are a pariah, unclean in blasphemy. Why should they wash you? Why should they feed you? Why should they give you something to drink? To them you are a problem about to be solved.

To me you are the Lord.

The city scarcely stirs, but here come the rulers with you in the midst. Serious faces. Where are they going? To the governor's forum. The Romans begin their work-day frightfully early, so the council is hurrying, lest they miss their chance for an audience and a quick imperial trial. Go! Go! They prod you from behind. Go, don't drag your feet! What's the matter with you? Tired? They themselves are filled with hectic energy. Sleeplessness has nerved them, and their purpose verges on frenzy. Go!

Jesus, how do you feel? What are you thinking? You don't talk. Your mouth has been closed for such a long time now. Last night, before the legal machinery caught hold of you and began to grind you in its wheels, you said your soul was sorrowful, even unto death—and then your eyes revealed the grief. I saw it. But now, in the dawn of your deathday, your face is expressionless. I can read nothing in your eyes. Jesus! Jesus! How do you feel right now? What moods contend within you? What worlds collide inside your soul? O Jesus, are you hating? Are you praying? Are you screaming silently? Are you thinking about me now?

You walk, step by weary step, from Jerusalem to Rome, around the world, from life to death, away, away. Away from me. Away from my knowing, into mystery. O Jesus, it terrifies me that you go so far away from me! Please, give me a sign! I really can't stand this not knowing. Give me some sign from your solitude, Lord, please, please, that you are thinking of me.

Lord Jesus, do you love me now?

✝ ✝ ✝

Wordlessly, Jesus answers:

The walking itself is the sign, child.

The loneliness which I have chosen, and the cross that closes it—these are signs that I love you ever. I have to leave you to love you best. I go where I want you never to go, precisely because I love you.

Can you say "Amen" to that?

THE TWENTY-SECOND DAY

SATURDAY

MARK 15:1-5

> And as soon as it was morning the chief priests, with the elders and scribes, and the whole council held a consultation; and they bound Jesus and led him away and delivered him to Pilate.
>
> Pilate asked him, "Are you the King of the Jews?"
>
> And he answered him, "You have said so."
>
> And the chief priests accused him of many things.
>
> And Pilate again asked him, "Have you no answer to make? See how many charges they bring against you."
>
> But Jesus made no further answer, so that Pilate wondered.

Things are changing, suddenly and then swiftly. But one thing does not change.

Look: they've changed the charge against the accused. This was the business of their early-morning consultation: they needed some charge that the governor would accept as a serious transgression of Roman code. "Blasphemy" is meaningless to those who don't honor God. And since Pontius Pilate scorns the people of his province, he'd ignore internal squabbles. But they need Pilate's attention because they need Pilate's decree. The death sentence is a jealously guarded right of Rome alone; and that's the thing they will not change: Jesus of Nazareth must be executed.

Therefore, the new charge is a capital offense. High

treason. Sedition: "He wants to make himself a king of the Jews."
To the Roman governor that means: "He's a leader of the
resistance against the empire." A zealot.

It works. They get his attention. They get their trial.

The proceedings open with the indictment by the plaintiff,
in this case officials of the Sanhedrin.

There follows, then, an examination by the imperial
magistrate, Pontius Pilate. He hears testimony first from the
witnesses and then from the accused. Usually, this would be
enough, and after consulting his legal advisors, Pilate would
render a verdict, the sentence to be executed immediately.

But things are changing.

When Pilate asks the accused, "Are you the King of the
Jews," Jesus gives a *qualified* assent: "You have said so."
Evidently, they define the title, "king," differently, and Pilate is
forced to return to the plaintiff for further interrogation.

But things are changing with terrible speed. For when
Pilate questions them a second time, the chief priests blow up
with a blizzard of accusations, "many things!" Suddenly the first
charge of treason is weakened in Pilate's estimate; he perceives
that the real cause of the chief priests' complaint is envy. So the
prisoner's word now carries more weight than it had heretofore,
and Pilate returns to question Jesus a second time.

But, whereas the chief priests rose up in noise, Jesus has
descended into silence. Precisely when his word would be
strongest to save himself, he offers no word at all.

"Have you no answer to make?" the governor asks,
marveling at the man. "Look how many charges they bring
against you!"

No. No answer. Rather, a resolute, dignified calm—which,
in fact, inclines Pilate in his favor; for the fanatics of his province
are acting fanatical again, displaying the qualities he despises,
but this man remains unruffled.

Things are changing. Pilate is contemplating a verdict of

innocence. The chief priests feel the wind turn against them. They need a new tactic—

† † †

But with you, O Lord, one thing never changed:
>Ironically, you and your accusers had the selfsame goal, and by your very silence, steadfastly, you went as it was written of you. Human beings strategized; human evil sent you to your cross. But something huger hovered over the occasion, something of your own volition:

Love.

THE TWENTY-THIRD DAY
MONDAY

MARK 15:6–11

> *Now at the feast he used to release for them one prisoner for whom they asked. And among the rebels in prison, who had committed murder in the insurrection, there was a man called Barabbas. And the crowd came up and began to ask Pilate to do as he was wont to do for them.*
>
> *And he answered them, "Do you want me to release for you the King of the Jews?" For he perceived that it was out of envy that the chief priests had delivered him up.*
>
> *But the chief priests stirred up the crowd to have him release for them Barabbas instead.*

Behold the people! Though they think themselves the force of the morning, in charge of things (by virtue of their numbers and their noise), they are in fact being put to a test which shall reveal the truth beneath their words, the reality beneath their self-assumptions and all their pretense.

Behold the nature of the breed!

A crowd has gathered at the Praetorium, a rabble, an obstreperous delegation of Judeans whose presence complicates Pilate's inclination to release Jesus. These crowds are volatile. Instead of a simple release, then, a choice is offered the people. Let the people feel in charge; let the people decide. The Governor will, according to a traditional Passover amnesty, free one prisoner. Which will it be—

Jesus of Nazareth?—whom they have falsely accused of treason against the Empire?

Or Barabbas?—treasonous in fact, one who committed murder for the cause?

If they choose the latter, their loyalties to the Empire (which Jesus is supposed to have offended) are revealed a vile sham, and these are no more than temporizing hypocrites, pretending any virtue to satisfy a private end.

But the Governor will release only one prisoner. Which will it be?

Jesus—who is the Son of the Father, who is the Kingdom of God come near unto them?

Or Barabbas—whose name means "the son of a (human) father," flesh itself, the fleshly pretensions to god-like, personal power in the kingdoms of the world?

This, precisely, is the timeless choice of humankind.

If they choose the latter, they choose humanity over divinity. They choose one who will harm them over one who would heal them.

If they choose Barabbas, they choose the popular revolutionary hero, the swashbuckler, the pirate, merry Robin Hood, the blood-lusty rake, the law-flout, violence glorified, appetites satisfied, James Bond, Billy Jack, Clint Eastwood, Rambo, the celebrated predator, the one who "turns them on," over one who asks them to "deny themselves and die." They choose (voluntarily!) entertainment over worship, self-satisfaction over sacrificial love, getting things over giving things, being served over serving, "feeling good about myself" and having it all and gaining the whole world and rubbing elbows with the rich rather than rubbing the wounds of the poor—

The choice is before them. And they think the choice is external, this man or that man. In fact, the choice is terribly internal: this nature or that one, good folks or people essentially selfish and evil, therefore. It's an accurate test of their character. How they choose is who they are.

Behold a people in desperate need of forgiveness.

† † †

And this, Christ, is the stunning irony:

that their evil was made good in you! You knew our nature as children of wrath; you knew exactly how we would choose; you put yourself in harm's way that our sin might kill you, that your death might redeem us even from our sinful nature!

Such knowledge is too wonderful for me; it is high, and I grow dizzy thinking about it. All that I can say with certainty, but with everlasting gratitude, is—

Amen.

THE TWENTY-FOURTH DAY

TUESDAY

❧

MARK 15:11–14

> *The chief priests stirred up the crowd to have him release for them Barabbas instead.*
>
> *And Pilate again said to them, "Then what shall I do with the man whom you call the King of the Jews?"*
>
> *And they cried out again, "Crucify him!"*
>
> *And Pilate said to them, "Why? What evil has he done?"*
>
> *But they shouted all the more, "Crucify Him!"*

Morning. The sun stands at the eastern horizon, hard and hot; the entire eastern sky is white with its shining. The wind is out of the northwest, but it comes uncertainly and sometimes turns back on itself. Little clouds like human hands are rising in the west.

Jerusalem is near the end of the rainy season. It might—but it might not—rain today. The sun is solid, but other elements in heaven are troubled and unpredictable. Animals all over the city stamp and shiver. They twist their ears to a distant sound. A roaring. Thunder, perhaps? The onset of storm? No, it is a human noise. A hundred throats are roaring at Gabbatha. There is a mob there demanding its will of the Governor—humanity, making its choice.

Pontius Pilate stands before this crowd, confounded. He had expected to ease their antagonisms by offering amnesty. If they didn't choose Jesus for release (he reasoned), yet they might forget him. And if they couldn't forget him, they might at least be satisfied to take Barabbas as a triumph of sorts and calm their violent temper.

Well, they didn't choose Jesus.

So Pilate asked them a question intended to test his success at cooling their mood. He said: "What'll I do with the fellow you call King of the Jews?"—and then he took three steps backward, gaping.

Whether he asked it wrong, or whether there's something deeper between the prisoner and the people than he can fathom, their thunderous answer stunned the governor. He stands now confounded, and all the beasts of Jerusalem shiver and stamp as before a storm. Such a roaring is shaking the morning! A hundred throats all bellowing one word.

Pilate glances left at the cause of this general fury—at Jesus of Nazareth, who stands solitary on the porch regarding this foaming sea of people, hearing (surely!) the horrible word they utter—and the governor shakes his head, bewildered. How could one man—?

"Why?" cries Pilate suddenly. He seriously means the question: "What evil has he done?"

But we are now at the climax of human hatreds. This rage requires no rationale. This hatred has no reason but itself. God and the children of Adam are enemies, for the children rebelled against their God—and enemies hate. That is enough to say. Treasons and charges and blasphemies are forgotten now. No answer is given Pilate's question. The question is pointless in the heat of ancient enmities.

"Why?" cries Pontius Pilate, but rage redoubles itself. The storm increases. That single word is repeated merely, roared and roared the louder: no proof, no premise, no logic to support it. For this is the natural reaction of sinners in the presence of Holy God, and its passion alone is its validity. They scream:

Crucify! Crucify! Crucify! Crucify! Crucify!

† † †

O Jesus:

You gazed into the hundred hearts amassed before you, thick with fear and fury. Was mine among them? Yes. Mine was among them. I have desired your death in order to preserve my life, my way of life, my fulfillments, and my own control.

But you, like me, desired your death too!

By a mercy I cannot comprehend, you accepted my evil intent even to save my life! Well, I am therefore my own no more, but yours—no more an enemy, a friend to you forever.

Lord Jesus, how I love you!

Amen.

THE TWENTY-FIFTH DAY
WEDNESDAY

MARK 15:15

So Pilate, wishing to satisfy the crowd, released for them Barabbas; and having scourged Jesus, he delivered him to be crucified.

The crowd is a power to be feared. In fact, its power *is* the fear it inspires in rulers who know its quickness to riot, its ungovernable lack of sense or of personal integrity.

People lose individuality in a crowd. At a certain flash-point they fuse into one simple bellowing brute, passionate and huge. A rioting crowd, then, can destroy a ruler's schemes, good or bad, a ruler's authority, the rule and the ruler together. Therefore, rulers satisfy crowds before they riot.

Jesus' enemies fear the crowd. That's why, as rulers, they would not arrest him in public. But they also appreciate the power of the crowd, and that's why, as citizens, they whip it to a frenzy in front of another ruler, the Roman Governor. They have no personal care for the people who compose the crowd. To them it's a beast of a hundred throats which they might ride to their own advantage (as long as it doesn't turn and kill them).

And Pilate fears the crowd. He sees the brute swell louder and huger. It's beginning to eat him up: it has ravaged justice and now devours whatever virtue this ruler might have had, spitting him out as a man of expedience only. To prevent a riot, Pontius Pilate satisfies the crowd. He releases Barabbas. He orders Jesus scourged. He delivers innocence to be crucified.

Thus the power of this brute: it swallows the soul of a Roman; it feeds on the body and blood of the Son of God.

Clearly, neither the high priests nor Pilate ever see the crowd as anything *but* a brute. Rulers don't find precious what they fear; they avoid it, or they use it, or they feed it. That's all.

But Jesus, even when he is food for the Many, sees the crowd as persons after all, individuals to be redeemed, sheep in need of a shepherd, captives to be freed, children, little children lost whom he came to seek and to save. If there's a brute about, that brute is Lucifer. Sin is brutal. But even the swollen-throated bellowers in the crowd are *people* to Jesus, whom he regards one by one by one, whom he does not fear, but whom he is serving right now—*right now!*—by giving his life to ransom them from the very brutishness they are displaying.

Ah, who can believe the paradox of our report? The crowd would destroy Jesus by crucifying him. But Jesus would destroy the crowd—by naming its persons one and one, by calling them out of the brute-slavery of sin, by loving them and renewing one by one their right spirit and their personhood.

Where there is a divine relationship with each individual soul, there can be no crowd. There is only a holy communion.

But he has to die first—

† † †

The righteous Servant shall cause many to be accounted righteous; for he pours out his soul unto death; he bears the sin of many and makes intercession for the transgressors. By dying, he kills the brute.

Jesus, you are like no human ruler. Never, never did a ruler look at me with such earnest singularity, such exclusive attention and mercy as you. I saw you, Jesus, seeing me. Across the heads of all the people, I saw your eyes on me.

I cannot speak.

THE TWENTY-SIXTH DAY
THURSDAY

MARK 15:16–20

> *And the soldiers led him away inside the palace (that is, the Praetorium); and they called together the whole battalion. And they clothed him in a purple cloak and plaiting a crown of thorns they put it on him.*
>
> *And they began to salute him, "Hail, King of the Jews!"*
>
> *And they struck his head with a reed and spat upon him, and they knelt down in homage to him. And when they had mocked him, they stripped him of the purple cloak, and put his own clothes on him.*
>
> *And they led him out to crucify him.*

Now the soldiers lead him away, inside the palace (that is, the Praetorium).

> *You have heard that it was said, "An eye for an eye and a tooth for a tooth." But I say to you, Do not resist one who is evil.*

And they call together the whole battalion, some six hundred soldiers, auxiliary troops recruited from the non-Jewish peoples of Palestine. "Recreation!" they cry. "A little R-and-R!"

> *If anyone strikes you on the right cheek, turn to him the other also.*

Jesus has already been scourged with the flagellum. His back is bleeding. When they pull a purple cloak across his shoulders, the blood soaks through. They weave a crown from the thorny branches of a nearby shrub. They stick this to his head, brow, and scalp.

> *You have heard that it was said, "You shall love your neighbor and hate your enemy." But I say to you, Love your enemies and pray for those who persecute you.*

The soldiers begin to salute him in a raucous mockery of high office, hooting, "Hail, you King of the Jews!"

> *For if you love those who love you, what reward have you? And if you salute your friends alone, what more are you doing than others? Even sinners do the same.*

And they strike his head with a reed, pitiful sign for a scepter.

> *Judge not, and you will not be judged.*

And they turn and spit on him.

> *Condemn not, and you will not be condemned.*

And they kneel down in grinning homage to him.

> *Forgive, and you will be forgiven.*

And when they've grown weary of the game, they strip him of the purple cloak (a mantle belonging to some nameless Roman soldier) and put his own clothes back on him.

> *Blessed are you when men revile you and persecute you and utter all kinds of evil against you falsely on my account. Rejoice and be glad, for your reward is great in heaven, for so men persecuted the prophets who were before you and . . .*

And so those who led him into the palace now lead him out again, to crucify him.

† † †

Sanctify me, Jesus!

> There is nothing you ask of me that you have not yourself exemplified. Nothing. Daily make me more like you.
>
> Amen.

PART FIVE

GOLGOTHA

THE TWENTY-SEVENTH DAY

FRIDAY

❦

MARK 15:20c–21

And they led him out to crucify him.

And they compelled a passer-by, Simon of Cyrene, who was coming in from the country, the father of Alexander and Rufus, to carry his cross.

I saw you walk in the early dawn to the Governor's palace. You were so tired then. Now you are torn. Your robe is stiffening with your own blood. Ah, my Lord!—they scourged you! Oh, my Lord. You will never lie down to sleep again.

Four soldiers and a Roman centurion lead you through the city. Such a tiny force. Scarcely noticeable. Who notices? It's mid-morning. The streets are crowded, citizens and merchants and the festival pilgrims, busy, busy, crying their wares in that high voice, indifferent to another execution. Who notices? I see the high priests amid the faces, moving parallel to you, making sure the deed gets done. And I see pockets of your friends peering from the side streets, startled and helpless. Women, mostly. And I am here. I notice.

The soldiers are impatient. They dart their eyes here and there through the throng. What do they expect? Or fear? Your eyes are half closed, your legs slow and leaden, your body caved around a rough piece of timber. You are carrying your own crossbeam at the stomach. You're dragging it beside your feet, moving with an awkward side-shuffling motion—pulling the thing! Another man would have heaved it onto his shoulders.

Not you. I know why not, and I hate this world: your back and sides have been ripped by the hooks of the whip. You can't even touch the flesh, let alone lay wood on it. You slouch over it, laboring. Once you walked upright, dignified. Now you shuffle, dust on your lips, shaking with exhaustion, hugging the wood as if it were a dying child. You'll never sleep again. Yet these soldiers are impatient. You move too slowly. Why don't they carry the crossbeam for you? Oh, I hate this world!

You stumble. A soldier yells at you. I am crying. I can't watch. I can't watch. People keep blocking my vision. Ah, God! The sun has risen halfway to heaven, dead-white, round, hot. There are some black clouds in the west. They're coming here to Jerusalem. I don't even feel the wind, but it's blowing and they are coming.

Oh, how can I *not* watch? How can I *not* be with you, Lord?

I've pushed myself right into the soldiers' path. I can be bold, because I love you. I make them notice me by standing in the way, and then I beg them, "Let me carry his cross. He can't! Let me."

One fool finds this amusing. "You're a woman," he tells me.

But another finds it practical and claps the closest pilgrim on the shoulder and commands him to take your cross and follow them out of the city. Oh, Jesus, but then I am left with nothing to do! Does that stranger understand the honor? You glance at him—I see this, my hand on my mouth—you glance at him when he lifts the beam from your arms. How dearly I long for such a glance! What can I do for you? Please look at me! Jesus, Jesus, what can I do for you now?

✝   ✝   ✝

Follow.

TWENTY-EIGHTH DAY

SATURDAY

MARK 15:22–23

And they brought him to the place called Golgotha (which means the place of a skull). And they offered him wine mingled with myrrh; but he did not take it.

As a sheep before her shearers is dumb, so Jesus has been silent. In Mark's account, he has revealed nothing of his private thought or his personal feeling since Gethsemane. He spoke a few words last night, and then again this morning; but these were responses to his inquisitors. His spirit has been mute. The body is before us; the mind is hidden in mystery.

But now, finally, on Golgotha, comes a spontaneous gesture, and with it an insight into the spirit of the Savior. We see what he's been doing in the solitude of his interior self.

Jesus, stripped of his clothes, is lying on his back, his head and hands arranged on the *patibulum*, the crossbeam by which they will lift him bodily to a thick post for execution. His eyes are shut. The wood beneath his head might seem a pillow; but soldiers stand with spikes beside him. They make a rough motion, a sign of assent, as if to say, *Now—but right now, or you miss the chance. Hurry!*

So then a woman rushes over and kneels by the figure of Jesus and offers him a drink. She's performing a merciful ritual, not unusual among the Jews: "Give strong drink to the dying," commands the thirty-first chapter of Proverbs, "and wine to those in bitter distress; let them drink and remember their misery no more." The woman is seeking to ease the torment of the crucifixion. She's offering Jesus myrrh, a narcotic.

And here is the gesture, revelation, the mind of the dying Christ:

He shakes his head. He will not drink from her cup. He will in no wise dull his senses or ease the pain.

And so we know. What are the feelings? What has the spirit of Jesus been doing since Gethsemane? Why, suffering. With a pure and willful consciousness, terribly sensitive to every thorn and cut and scornful slur: suffering. This he has chosen. This he is attending to with every nerve of his being—not for some perverted love of pain. He hates the pain. But for a supernal love of us, that pain might be transfigured, forever.

Or what has the Lord been doing since Gethsemane? Drinking. Not from the woman's narcotic cup, but from the cup the Father would not remove from him: drinking. Swallow by swallow, tasting the hell therein, not tossing it down in a hurry: "So that by the grace of God he might taste death for every one."

Or what has the Lamb been doing since Gethsemane? Bearing our griefs. Carrying our sorrows. By the stripes he is truly and intensely receiving, healing us all.

† † †

And yet it pleased the Lord to bruise you! He has put you to grief, O my Jesus; your soul was made an offering for my sin, but then behold: I am an offspring of your sacrifice. For by it, I am born again.

Amen.

THE TWENTY-NINTH DAY
MONDAY

MARK 15:24a
And they crucified him.

If death is the end of all we do, then all we do is futile. Ask Ozymandias, king of kings, if you can find that mighty man—or if you remember him at all.

We may deny death. Indeed, we may be able, for a while, to ignore our personal dyings altogether by attending to the present day: *here* we are and *now* we are, no need to think what we will (or will not) be. Or we may romanticize our grander passions into something timeless, pieces of ourselves that must last forever (as poets call their verses deathless, as lovers can't conceive such love as theirs to die). We may philosophize our immortality by the arrogant, god-like presumption that simply because we are—and because we are aware that we are—we cannot *not* be.

But if death waits at the ends of our lives to end them, it cancels not just the next day nor just the continuance of living: it swallows the whole life, even back to its beginning. Suddenly we are not, as though we never had been. There are those who console themselves that history, at least, will remember them. (Ozymandias was such a one.) But if death is the end of human endeavor—and so of humanity—then who will remember history?

Oh, people: if death defines us, so that we who came from nothing also go back to nothing, then death is a worm that curls inside our every act, like a parasite eating the lasting value out of it! Even in our dearest kissing is the parasite which shall, on our deathday, prove that this act, too, was futile, and all our loving so much sound and fury, signifying nothing.

The planets, their civilizations and their loads of people, all need a central sun—to hold them together, to keep them wheeling in good order, to bequeath them shape and meaning. History needs a center. But if that center is empty death, strengthless death, it cannot hold. Things fly apart into absurdity. Finally, every deed is hollow, ourselves mere spasms in a mindless infinity, and all our glorious history remembered only so long as it is; forgotten, when it is not, forever: a nothing. A vanity. We are the dreams the comets can't recall. We were, for a while, a walking dust.

But the Creator God put a cross in the very center of human history—to *be* its center, ever.

The Son of God, the gift of God, the love of God, the endless light of the self-sufficient God filled the emptiness which was death at our core. People, here is eternal life in the very midst of us!

Now, therefore, it is the person and the passion of Jesus Christ which defines us; and because of him we go no longer down to nothing: our end is the beginning of a perfect union with God, the Beginner Of Everything.

Behold, this is the central event of the whole of history; behold, this is the sun that keeps the planets and bequeaths importance to the peoples and makes significant even me and all I do: *And they crucified him.* It happened. Eternity entered time. They crossed at the cross.

We are altogether meaningless, except God touch us. God touched us here.

We fly into an infinity of hell, separated from life and from each other and from divinity forever, except God hold us. God holds us here.

† † †

My dear ones,
>   *I kiss you—and my kiss is pure and good. It lasts for you forever. Because my love is strong and bright and rich and true and worthy forever.*
>
>   Because my Savior is.

THE THIRTIETH DAY
TUESDAY

MARK 15:24–28

And they crucified him.

They divided his garments among them, casting lots for them to decide what each should take. It was the third hour when they crucified him.

The inscription of the charge against him read, "The King of the Jews."

With him they crucified two robbers, one on his right and one on his left.

I stand apart. I draw no one's attention. I have covered my head. These are the things I see:

I see four soldiers upon a low hill, their greater labor done, their duty now to wait. They are hunching over the few benefits of the morning's assignment. That is, by a grim tradition they can keep the final possessions of those they crucify; so now they're casting lots for an undergarment, a robe, a belt, sandals. No money here. Not even a scrip. No matter: the soldiers are passing time. It's nearly noon.

A centurion stands over them with his arms folded, gazing up at a coming thunderhead of cloud, squinting, figuring.

Above the soldiers, above the centurion, but yet beneath the sun and the lowering cloud, hang three men on crosses, each of them stripped to a loin cloth: a robber, a robber, and you.

The wind is picking up. Dust blows by. And this is what I see:

A wooden board is nailed roughly over your head, chalk-white and burned with the indictment: "The King of the Jews." I say, *Yes!* In my soul I cry, *Yes! Yes!* I keep my face impassive for fear of the centurion and the chief priests, but *Yes*, I say, *it is what we've called Messiah: King of the Jews!* The loutish Romans are right. They mean to mock us, to mock all the Jews as a single people, but their scorn tells the truth, and I take a bitter satisfaction in it. Let the chief priests burst their bellies with indignation—I'll just laugh! I hate this world.

But if you're the Messiah, why are you crucified? How can this be? Jesus, Jesus, Jesus, forgive me. My mind rejects the things I see. Nothing fits! I call you King. I call you Master and Lord. You *are* the Lord! No one has loved as you do—no, not ever, Lord. But I never imagined Goodness to be so broken. Jesus, you grieve me! Jesus, you confuse me—

This is what I see:

Your knees keep buckling. You push yourself up with your legs—to breathe, I think—but the legs lose strength and pop at the knees, and your body drops, hah! The arms stretch. The hands clutch spikes. Your shoulder-joints separate. Your muscles draw out like ropes. Your rib-cage splays. I can count the bones! How do you breathe when your chest is stretched flat? Jesus, you're not breathing! Your own body, when it drags on your arms like that—why, your own weight is suffocating you!

Breathe!

Sweet Jesus, please! Breathe!

Make fists on the spike-heads! Lift yourself up. Open your mouth, Lord Jesus, please! Don't die. Don't stop breathing! Breathe! Breathe! What? What are you—? Oh, no—

No, no, no, don't do that, not now, not while you hang so low, not in surrender, no: *Jesus, don't look at me! Don't look at me like that!* I can't stand it if you look at me. My whole body burns like fire. You make me too much here! You're wasting yourself. You should fight for your life, Lord! You cannot die. Rise up! Rise up on your arms! Fight! Fight! Breathe—

† † †

But the eyes of Christ ask, "*Do you take offense at this?*"

There were times when I begged for your glance because I needed to know your love, that you loved me. But you did not so much as lift your eyes; I lacked the signs of your presence and your affection, and I felt abandoned. So then I was angry.

Now you look directly at me, and I feel sick with my own presence, immediate, real, astonishing over the ages: and my shame. O Jesus, does love from the cross have to hurt so much?—hurt you with dying?—hurt me when your dying draws me to yourself? Why is it *now* that you gaze at me?

"*Do you take offense at this? Do you also wish to go away?*"

THE THIRTY-FIRST DAY
WEDNESDAY

MARK 15:29–31

> *And those who passed by derided him, wagging their heads and saying, "Aha! You who would destroy the temple and build it in three days, save yourself and come down from the cross!"*
>
> *So also the chief priests mocked him to one another with the scribes, saying, "He saved others; he cannot save himself. Let the Christ, the King of Israel, come down now from the cross, that we may see and believe."*
>
> *Those who were crucified with him also reviled him.*

Is it nothing to you, all ye that pass by? Behold, and see if there be any sorrow like unto my sorrow, which is done unto me, wherewith the Lord hath afflicted me in the day of his fierce anger.

No, there never was such sorrow as this. And the fools who pass by jeering merely reveal an iniquitous ignorance. Passers-by indeed! Untouched, absolutely insensitive: here are the unbelievers of the world.

The chief priests, on the other hand, are those who should know better, having learned the Word of God, but who seek herein nothing other than the proofs of their own power. Therefore they see only so much sorrow as they think they have themselves imposed, and they are (like all ecclesiastics seeking authority) satisfied by the crucifixion. Those crucified with him

121

know no more than the priests (why should they?) and find in him but a little diversion on their way to death and perdition.

The sorrow of the Messiah is nothing to these; so they mock.

But we, who in steadfast faith do hear his cry—what sort of sorrow do we see? How painful is this mockery?

Well, if he is innocent, the mockery wounds him with tolerable wounds since he can wrap himself in the dignity and self-pity of a misunderstood goodness. If he is innocent, the crucifixion makes him a *better* man after all, since his sacrifice is the very extremity of selfless love. But if he is guilty, the mockery is accurate and right, and its wounds are an intolerable anguish.

Guilty? Is this thinkable, that Jesus is guilty? No, it is not thinkable. It is as unthinkable as the pain such guilt must cause—but it is true! There are moments right now when Jesus looks down on the sick derision of the people at his feet and he agrees: *It is right. I am worse than false priests and outright criminals.*

Who can fathom the grief of the Holy One of God, when he must say in his soul: *I deserve this.* Yet that, exactly, is the sorrow before us now.

Maybe none shall see with more terrible clarity the sorrow of our Lord than the apostle Paul: "For our sake," he writes, "God made him to be sin who knew no sin, so that in him we might become the righteousness of God" (2 Corinthians 5:21). He does not write: "To bear our guilt," as though a good man became better by substituting himself for our punishment. Severely, Paul writes, "God made him to *be* sin." Jesus has become a bad man, the worst of all men, the badness, in fact, *of* all men and all women together. Paul does not write, "To bear our sin," as though Jesus and sin are essentially separate things, the one a weight upon the other for a while. No, but "to *be* sin": Jesus is sin! Jesus is the thing itself!

Today, Friday, between the third hour and the ninth, beneath a blackening sky, Jesus has become the rebellion of humankind against its God.

He is, therefore, rightly crucified. He bows before his deserving. There is nothing to ease his sorrow—no, not even some sweet internal sense of innocence. However mistaken the motives of his enemies, Jesus belongs on the cross because sin deserves—sin requires!—the complete, judicial damnation of the Deity.

And yet, and yet: this same Jesus is also the Holy One of God, now as much as ever before—because now he is completely obedient to the Father. Holy, he must hate sin with an unyielding hatred. Behold, then, and see a sorrow unlike any other sorrow in the universe: that right now Jesus hates himself with an unyielding hatred.

He is, in his own eyes, vile. He cannot console himself with the goodness of his sacrifice or the wickedness of his detractors, passers-by, priests, criminals—because they are right! The wicked ones are right.

This is, perhaps, the second bitterest swallow in the cup of suffering which he drinks.

The worst is yet to come.

† † †

This, Christ?
> Is it from such anguished self-knowledge as this that you have saved me?—the deep knowing of my own sinfulness, a knowing from the vantage of the Judge, my unrighteousness in God's most righteous eyes? Self-loathing for eternity? Hell, therefore?

> Yes. Because in you I have become the righteousness of God.

> Yes! Amen.

THE THIRTY-SECOND DAY
THURSDAY

MARK 15:33–34

> *And when the sixth hour had come, there was darkness over the whole land until the ninth hour. And at the ninth hour Jesus cried with a loud voice, "Eloi, Eloi, lama sabachthani?"—which means, "My God, my God, why hast thou forsaken me?"*

Noon. The sun at its zenith is hidden.

That great, black, frowning range of cloud from the west has killed the sunlight, closed the sky, swallowed the earth in a yellow darkness. The wind is still. The city stops breathing. Animals grow so restive they rear against their traces, rolling their eyes. Owners shout through the darkness the names of the beasts. Parents stand in stone doorways and cry out for their children: *Miriam! Yeshy? Yeshy?*

There descends from heaven a long, low muttering. Another. The commanders of the elements are taking counsel together.

Suddenly, lightning! The crack shatters the dark: blinding light, a splitting sound—as a cedar twists and screams and breaks from its trunk and tumbles down—and the boom of that thunder batters the houses of Jerusalem.

Yeshy! Yeshua, come home now! Now!

"And it shall come to pass in that day, saith the Lord God, that I will cause the sun to go down at noon, and I will darken the earth in the clear day . . . and I will make it as the mourning for an only son and the end thereof as a bitter day."

BOOM! The rain dots the dust with big drops. *BOOM!* Now it falls hard and straight and heavy. *BOOM!* The wind screams down and hurls raindrops like pellets flat-out at the faces of running human beings, stinging flesh. The black between the lightning is the darkness Egypt knew, thick darkness, even a darkness which may be felt.

Yeshua! Yeshua! Where are you? This is a pure, bloody panicking. But the weeping child cannot be heard. The weeping parents weep in vain.

BOOM!

No human mockery can match the voice of the storm for mortal scorn. Lightning flashes. The hill outside the city is white-wet and empty. Silhouettes stutter and black out: three crosses, the guards, some women at a distance. Those who laughed at the central figure this morning are gone. No one is laughing now.

Thus the first hour of the afternoon, and the second, and the third.

The few who stood the storm are still on the hill at the end of three hours—the ninth hour of the day. The lightning has fled. The thunder has exhausted itself. But the blackness persists—and suddenly a voice worse than thunder, because it is a human voice, a horrified wailing, arises: *Eloi! Eloi! My God! My God!*

Who is that? The one in the center. The one in the perfect center of elemental darkness, the focus of this storm, him: *Eloi! Lama sabach-thani?* Jesus of Nazareth, King of the Jews, him. He hangs in an abyss, that one. Him.

My God, why hast thou forsaken me?

Who answers him?

The thunder is silent. The city holds its breath. The heavens are shut. The dark is rejection. This silence is worse than death. No one answers him. No, not even God. Not even

God, his Father, because he who has become hateful in his own eyes now is hateful likewise to God, his Father.

Jesus. Him. It is against *him* that heaven has been shut.

In this terrible moment of storm, the loss of light for humanity is at once the loss of love and life for its Christ. He has entered the absolute void. Between the Father and the Son now exists a gulf of impassable width and substance. It is the divorce of despising. For, though the Son still loves the Father obediently and completely, the Father despises the Son completely because he sees in him the sum of human disobedience, the sum of it from the beginning of time to the end of time. He hates the Son, even unto damning him.

This is a mystery, that Christ can be the obedient, glorious love of God and the full measure of our disobedience, both at once. But right now this mystery is also a fact. And the fact must seem to last forever. Hell's horror is that it lasts forever.

And this, precisely, is the bitterest drop in the cup: that, crying down eternity unheard, separated absolutely from God—from the God he cannot help but love even still—Jesus is in Hell. The darkness that covers Jerusalem from noon to the middle of the afternoon, it is no less than the damnation of the Messiah, who wails and gnashes his teeth in an utter solitude from now (so it must seem) unto eternity. Hell is eternal. And he has descended into Hell.

† † †

But your iniquities have separated you and your God, and your sins have hid his face from you, that he will not hear.

No, my sins.

But you, my Savior, were my sins before the Father.

Then this, too, is what you have saved me from: the cold rejection of the living God, a wandering solitude forever and ever. Hell is colder than the promise of it is hot. Hell is zero in the bone of the universe.

You saved me from damnation.

Thank you, Jesus!

THE THIRTY-THIRD DAY
FRIDAY

MARK 15:34–36

> And at the ninth hour Jesus cried with a loud voice, "Eloi, Eloi, lama sabach-thani?" which means, "My God, my God, why hast thou forsaken me?"
>
> And some of the bystanders hearing it said, "Behold, he is calling Elijah."
>
> And one ran and, filling a sponge full of vinegar, put it on a reed and gave it to him to drink, saying, "Wait. Let's see whether Elijah will come to take him down."

Shh! Be quiet! Listen! Who is that?

Listen: somebody's running. You can hear the mud-guzzled footsteps. A fast potching sound. You just can't *see*. It's too dark to see. It's night in the midst of the afternoon.

And who could understand the cry of "the King of the Jews," Jesus of Nazareth, him in the middle? Nobody knows his trouble. No one can make sense of that wailing: *Eloi! Eloi!*

But someone's running downhill, toward the supplies the soldiers brought. A man—it might be a woman—squats. A splashing, a thrusting of something into liquid in a jug. Then dripping—pulling something out of the liquid again. Holding it over the surface, drip, drip. Ha! Do you know what you're hearing?

The dark figure now lifts a long stick—a staff? a reed, perhaps?—from the shadows on the hillside, and rises, and runs back toward the central cross, all the while trying to balance a floppy object the size of a hand on the end of the stick, murmuring, "Wait, wait." The whispering figure extends the stick up to the beard, up to the mouth of Jesus. "Here. Drink this."

Well! Do you understand? In the middle of his agony, someone seeks to soothe him. It's a sponge, sopped full of vinegar, a sour wine. It's a pitifully poor medicinal, to be sure, but a gesture of kindness nonetheless—and the best this minister could think of.

And, as Jesus makes hungry sucking sounds at the sponge, the good Samaritan says, "Let's see if Elijah will come to take him down." An empty piety, a very old legend: that the prophet would rescue righteous people in their distress. Worse than empty, it's a blunt misunderstanding of Jesus' cry and of his passion—of Jesus himself. Nonetheless, it is the desire of a kind soul, however ignorant.

Who is this? Who responds with such a pitiful ministration? There was a woman who tried to give him this same drink six hours ago, just before they hoisted him aloft. He refused then. He accepts now.

Whose gift has he accepted?

Is this that woman again? Or a man? A Roman (but what Roman would know even the rude legends about Elijah)? A Jew, then (but what Jew would *not* understand "Eloi" in his native Aramaic)? Neither Jew nor Roman? A stranger, maybe? An enigma, surely. A puzzle, so far as the story goes: one by nature blind to the nature of Christ, believing more fervently in pious legends, but kind. Kind, withal. Moved to pity and to serve another's suffering. A helpless, hopeless sympathizer. A human, indeed. Humanity itself, perhaps, caught in a dismal daytime night. Yes, yes: it is you. It is your gift, your effort, your heart, you.

You, in your worldly form, before your second birth, the

very one whom Jesus came to save, here serving him to the best of your human ability—kind, withal.

You.

† † †

I do not know you, Jesus. Not wholly.

But you know me altogether. You knit me in my mother's womb. And anywhere I might go, in body or in spirit, there are you ahead of me.

Perhaps we people will ever be strangers in part and puzzles to one another, always a little lonely. But you, Lord, have searched me and known me. You have searched and loved and saved me even in my ignorance. I was a nice guy—but nice merely, kind only, and dying, till you died for me. More than water, then, and more than vinegar.

All praise to you!

Amen.

THE THIRTY-FOURTH DAY
SATURDAY

MARK 15:37–39a

> *And Jesus uttered a loud cry and breathed his last.*
>
> *And the curtain of the temple was torn in two, from top to bottom.*
>
> *And when the centurion who stood facing him saw that he thus cried out and breathed his last—*

"A loud cry." In Greek the words are *phone megale*, which, transposed, begin to look familiar: a *mega-phone*.

A shout of triumph!

† † †

Under other circumstances, this centurion commands a hundred fighting men, not four at a quick execution. He ranks with sixty brother-centurions in a legion of six thousand troops. He stands nowhere near the top of that brotherhood, but he isn't a grunt, he isn't the boy at the bottom.

So who is this "King of the Jews"? And why does his crucifixion require such attention? The storm cleared the hill of all but some women; no one's attacked; no one threatens to "save" the crucified. No one, friend or foe, has endured the last three hours of furious skies. Apparently, fear of darkness is stronger than hate for this man. Or love. So what's the point? The centurion has stuck it out. But why a *centurion*, after all?

No complaints, of course. None registered, at least. This

commander is aging. He's waiting his pension. He does what's wanted.

See to it, Centurion!

I'll see to it, sir.

And so he has seen to it over the years. Forced marches down stone roads, keeping the troops both tight and stepping; fighting hand-to-hand in the provinces. Not wars, really. Nations don't challenge Rome these days—but there were battles of immediate noise and blood and danger and intensity. He had heard men die. He had heard the thick, liquid gargle of a final cry in blood. They drowned in it. He had heard the best of them whimper when pain overwhelmed courage, and they broke. Or they cursed—not in hatred, just in explosive comment on the suffering. Thrashed and cursed. Said, "Kill me, kill me, kill me, kill me—" And he has answered more than a few with a word from his *gladium*. The sword can honor a dying man. A dying soldier. Not a criminal.

I'll see to it, sir.

And so he has lingered through a truly terrifying storm, a blackness three hours long, here on a hill, exposed to the wind's lash, protecting . . . what? Whom? Who is this Jesus? The rain runs his body in rivulets, beard and hair stuck to flesh, head bent backward, upward. The rim of his top teeth shows. Whereas his companions have begun shivering and crying in the cold, till now he has held his peace. One curses. One weeps. Common responses. The man in the middle flares his nostrils and groans.

Then, just in the last minutes, he breathed deeply, he swelled his chest and bellowed a hoarse word: "Eloi, Eloi—" something. Can't translate. But this, finally, is what the centurion expects. Right about now, six hours into the torment, even the best begin to break. Okay, then: so this Jesus of Nazareth is no different from everyone else who—

What was that?

A loud shout! *Phone megale!* What? What? No, this is not at all what the centurion expects. It's a cry that he has heard before, to be sure—but never in defeat and never, never in

131

death, always when the soldier has won the battle or the king the war!

This is a cry of triumph!

The centurion whirls around to see Jesus: he sees eyes like fiery darts in the darkness; he sees a mouth thin and thin, as thin as the blade of a sword, grinning!

Victorious? King of the Jews—victorious over what? What do these flaming eyes announce?

Satan, thou art defeated in my defeat! Sin, dispossessed of a people! Death, look about thee; thou art not mighty and dreadful. Lo, I close my eyes and die—and death shall be no more.

Then, suddenly, he dies. The centurion's jaw drops. He stares, but he's seen it before; he knows the signs: Jesus is dead. Dead. No coma, no deeper sleep than another sleep. All at once the eyes see nothing, the mind thinks nothing, the heart has ceased to beat—

—but *suddenly!* That's what rivets the centurion. It is as if this man chose to go fully conscious straight to the wall of death, and there to strike it with all his might and, in the striking, die. Aware of absolutely everything.

See to it, Centurion.

I'll see to it all, sir.

No, not all. One thing astounds the centurion: how can a crucified criminal act so convincingly like the victor?

† † †

O Christ!

When you died, you broke the wall that divided us from God: you struck it, you cracked it, you tore it apart—you made a door of that which had been death before.

And the sign was that "the veil of the temple was rent in twain, from the top to the bottom," and the mercy seat was made open to my approach.

Amen.

THE THIRTY-FIFTH DAY
MONDAY

MARK 15:39

And when the centurion who stood facing him saw that he thus cried out and breathed his last, he said, "Truly, this man was the Son of God!"

The centurion whirls around and sees Jesus, so suddenly dead upon that battle cry of triumph—sees the central criminal with such stunning clarity, sees as he has never seen before—and whispers with the solemn weight of a personal confession, whispers in a late day's dawning, "Truly, this man—"

Here is a paradox, both impossible and true.

Jesus is rejected by God, is cut completely off from God, is hung on a tree and thereby cursed, divorced at all points from his Father. *And yet:* it is in this same Jesus, at this same moment, precisely *because of* his sacrifice and death, that God is most present to the world! It is in Jesus *on the cursed tree* that God's supreme intentions toward the world are made manifest: that he hasn't come to curse, but rather to love and to bless.

God is not here with Jesus. Yet God is indeed here, in Christ, reconciling the world unto himself!

God and his sin-corrupted Son are as removed from one another as hell is from heaven.

Yet the whole passion is of holy design! Cursing is integral to that design. And the Father, verily absent, is also verily here, accepting the sacrifice.

This once we can have it both ways and can delight in the

manic breaking of the rules of the universe. This once the creatures, we created ones, can rise up *in* creation to peer *beyond* creation through a magic window at the Uncreated One, the Creator. Here is a window through which to gaze into Heaven, to know and believe in the nature of God. Here, in paradox. Here, in the conjunction of impossibilities. Here, on Golgotha.

And here is a door through which God has crossed infinity to enter our finite existence, flooding the dungeons with light. Here is a door through which we by faith may enter Heaven, a doorway made of nails and wood, a crossing, a cross.

But deepen further this paradox. Ask: when were the windows most darkened for Jesus, that he could see nothing of God the Father? Answer: On Golgotha. And by what was the great door bolted shut and locked against his entering in? By the wood and the nails of the cross.

Christ's unseeing *is* our sight.

His solitude is the beginning of human communion with God.

For it is on Golgotha that a centurion spins around and stares at the man in the middle, just as that man dies, exactly as Jesus gives up the ghost and slumps forward from the cross.

But all at once that centurion sees as though light burst upon his eyes, as though the veil between bright heaven and dark earth had been torn in two from the top to the bottom. The centurion sees better than he did, and more than he ever did before: he sees God! He sees the very nature of the love of God! The dying of one is the other one's window, and what has been veiled is now revealed, and a pagan whispers with the solemn weight of conviction, confession, faith: "Truly, this man was the Son of God!"

† † †

For God so loved the world that he gave his only Son, that whoever believes in him should not perish but have eternal life. And this "giving"—this giving *up*, this giving *away*, this giving *over*—began indeed in Bethlehem in a cradle made of wood. But it wasn't done till he was killed by a cross of wood on Golgotha.

Because of the window and the door, O Lord, my dearest love and adoration are yours now and forever.

Amen.

THE THIRTY-SIXTH DAY
TUESDAY

MARK 15:40–41

There were also women looking on from afar, among whom were Mary Magdalene, and Mary the mother of James the younger and of Joses, and Salome, who, when he was in Galilee, followed him and ministered to him; and also many other women who came up with him to Jerusalem.

Jesus, look at you! Ahh, my Jesus, how will you ever say my name again? This day has been so sad, so long, so awful—but I wish to God it weren't over! Look at you, look at you, my Lord!

I saw you early this morning, more weary than the centuries since Abraham—since Adam. My heart broke. I said, *What is he thinking? Does he love me now?*

I saw you stumble out of the city, so torn by the whip that you could not lift the cross-beam or drag it behind you, but grabbed it at your stomach. Your blood-soaked robe! I started to cry.

I saw you dying. I saw you sunk between the wings of your own arms—and then you looked at me. You recognized me among the people. You gazed at me. You killed me, Jesus, with your eyes. You killed me, and I stopped crying. I grew cold and dead, and nothing mattered, and I have stayed through the storm. The soldiers for duty. I for . . . for love, for fear, and for this—that I have nothing else apart from you, nothing. I stayed. I stay. I am here. I am watching.

A little light, a dreary sort of grey light, is returning now after the storm. The wind is freshening. But it's the end of the day, really. My day. Our day. You departed in the darkness. You are dead. Look at you.

You lean from the straight wood. High go your arms, numb to the spikes, high like wings reaching the wind, but empty; your body is pitched forward from the pinch of your shoulders behind; your head is bowed down to earth; your hair is a rain around your face, limp and lifted by this fresher wind. Oh, Jesus, your head hangs so low that I can see the flesh of your back. I can see the whip-wounds, like mouths: open and tongueless and white and, Jesus, silent, Jesus, Jesus! Jesus! How can the world be the same without you? Jesus! This silence shrieks at me. How can people stroll down the wet roads as if nothing has changed? You are dead! My heart that you shamed in me, my heart is dead—huge and heavy and stone-dead, and I can't even cry.

Salome is crying. I envy her. The other Mary is holding her: two old women bent against each other, weeping. I want to be old. I want to be almost dead. I want to *be* dead! I don't want to *be!* Oh, I don't want any of this to be. I want to scream it all away and—gone! Gone! The cross and the hill and the city, the sky and the day—gone! I want to slap those smug people strolling by. Jesus! Jesus! You are so dead!

But I love you.

But I will never hear you say my name again.

O Jesus, you will never walk from a morning mist, fresh from your Father, reaching to me and murmuring my name. You will never say, *Peace*, to me again. You will never say, *Mary*—

† † †

Grief, while you are grieving, lasts forever. But under God, forever is a day.

Weeping, darling Magdalene, may last the night. But joy cometh with the sunrise—and then your mourning shall be dancing, and gladness shall be the robe around you. Wait.

Wait.

PART SIX

THE
GARDEN
OF TOMBS

THE THIRTY-SEVENTH DAY
WEDNESDAY

MARK 15:42–43

> *And when evening had come, since it was the day of Preparation (that is, the day before the Sabbath), Joseph of Arimathea, a respected member of the council, who was also himself looking for the kingdom of God, took courage and went to Pilate and asked for the body of Jesus.*

Things are changing—immediately, though few can see the changes, and marvelously. People are not the same. One and one, at the death of the Christ. . . .

A centurion confesses the divinity of the crucified in terms he learned in Rome, *Son of God!*

A disciple still lingers near the cross to mourn her master, she herself changed only to a deeper sorrow, but she's a sign of how swiftly the word goes forth, how suddenly the radical effect of the Christ begins, because she, with the women, is still on Golgotha when Joseph returns for the corpse.

Jesus dies mid-afternoon.

Joseph gets there before sundown!

But by sundown, Joseph of Arimathea is not as he has been. He has just negotiated a most complex and audacious request of Pontius Pilate, and he's changed.

One and one, at the death of the Christ—

Here is a respected member of the council, a man who was never a maverick. His reputation's solid. He has been looking for the kingdom of God, the right spirit of righteous people who delight in the Law. But suddenly he wants to act like *family* to the executed criminal! He wants the body! Who cares to bury the bodies of those utterly outcast from society? Only kin. What, is Joseph suddenly some sort of kin? He's changing.

And more than mere courtesy, his request is an act of personal courage. First, he will raise grave doubts in the whole Sanhedrin regarding himself: our brother Joseph, "He who is not with us—" and so forth.

Second, he risks the Governor's flat denial, and then what shall he have gained? On principle Rome refuses burial to those executed for high treason. And high treason's precisely the charge the council chose to pin on Jesus, according to which Pilate granted the sentence of death. (Unless Joseph perceives in Pilate some other, softer attitude toward the deceased: pity? Guilt? Regret? In which case he might break custom and release the body; in which case, how many are changing, and who, after all?—and so forth.)

Third, more than denial, he risks the wrath of the Roman. This is the second request in a single day from someone on the council. The first was granted against the Governor's will, forced by a roaring multitude; and Joseph would consider that first request—as long as he wants to stay in good standing with the council—the primary one: capital punishment. Crucifixion. Kill the criminal! Pilate was backed into a corner. Surely to switch feelings for Jesus, suddenly to desire the kind thing for him, risks the fury that Pilate could not have expressed before.

Joseph of Arimathea—he's acting like a maverick! A very bold maverick! He's walking away from the mind, the embrace, the identity, power, position, and comfort of the council. He's changing!

Somebody mutters: "No, he wants that body underground because a corpse uncovered on the Sabbath offends the law"— meaning, he isn't changing at all, and so forth. But if Joseph were only concerned for the Sabbath Bans (and not for Jesus particularly) he'd leave well enough alone. He'd leave corpses on crosses and councils quite satisfied and angry Romans to their own emotions.

But he enters the palace in spite of the risk. All by himself. He asks for the very body which the council despised and rejected not half a day ago, mocked, reviled, misused, and murdered: *That one, yes. Yes, he is dead. Jesus of Nazareth. That one. Him.*

Joseph is not the same. There's some new seeing in this kingdom-seeker. A veil's been torn, a wall breached, a window opened. Perhaps he's bold because he hopes. Perhaps he hopes because he's seen a more permanent splendor than ever before, the glory of the Lord.

Things are changing: it has an immediate, marvelous power, the glory of the Lord.

† † †

One thing I know: that though I was born blind, now I see.

Jesus said to me, *Do you believe in the Son of God?*

I said, Who is he, that I may believe in him?

Jesus said, *You have seen him, and it is he who speaks to you—*

I look, O Lord, even now, and I believe, and I do worship you.

Amen.

THE THIRTY-EIGHTH DAY
MAUNDY THURSDAY

MARK 15:44–45

And Pilate wondered if he were already dead; and summoning the centurion, he asked him whether he was already dead.

And when he learned from the centurion that he was dead, he granted the body to Joseph.

"Jesus of Nazareth?" says Pilate.

"Yes."

"Dead already?"

"Yes, sir."

"Crucified and died in—what? Six hours?"

"He was scourged first. He lost blood."

"So who doesn't get scourged? It still takes three days to die! And I saw this Jesus. A young man, intense and healthy, right? He was not weak. Clear-eyed, self-controlled, steadfast. Six hours?"

"There was a storm, sir."

"I know. I live here."

"A strange storm. A really dreadful storm, sir."

"So, then! Exposure killed the King of the Jews! Or maybe Jupiter of Thunderbolts. So the others are dead too, right?"

"No. They're alive."

"Right. And so is Jesus of Nazareth. No. You can't have his body. We're civilized. We bury the dead, sir, not the living. Get out."

"I promise you upon my honor that the man has died."

"You're a physician?"

"No, sir."

"Then Jesus is sleeping. He's *soporifer*. Comatose, you understand? This Rabbi found a way to beat the pain—and you too, by the looks of it. Get out."

"Governor, I could prove his death, but there's so little time. It's almost sunset. I beg you to believe me. Jesus is dead. Dead and dead and he must be buried. He can't be above when the sun goes down! Can I pay you? Can I buy the body, sir? I have money. What do you want? My rank? I'll give you my rank on the counsel. I give it *away!* Believe me—"

"Shut up."

"—I touched his flesh, as cold as clay—"

"*Shut up!* I'm tired of the business! I am tired of the day and the Jews and your thousand certitudes, your incomprehensible passions, wild-eyed, fanatic. You're all so . . . religious! Shut up, Joseph of Arimathea. Shut up. Get out."

"No."

"What?"

"No. I can't leave. Not without his body. No."

"*Raca!* You idiot! *Fatue!* Do you know what I can do to you? Did you see what I did to your King?"

"You killed him."

"*I did not kill him!* He is not dead! But I can kill you!"

"It doesn't matter. I'm sorry, sir, but it really doesn't matter. Apart from him I am nothing anyway. I want to bury my Lord in dignity, with honor. Except for that, you can take whatever you want from me. Take my life!"

"We are Romans! We do not bury the living!"

"He is dead. There is no breath in his pale corpse. The blood is thickening in his extremities. He is dead."

"Where's that centurion? Bring the officer in charge of the day's execution. Now! You, Joseph, shut up. Wait and say nothing. I'll believe those *paid* to be honest. Besides, that old soldier's about to be pensioned, nothing to gain in a lie—and what do you think he thinks of your Jewish religious involutions? Right. We'll both defer to a pragmatist, a Roman—"

And so there appears before the Governor a solid centurion: clear-eyed, controlled, immovable. Steadfast.

"Yes, sir," he says, "Jesus of Nazareth is dead."

And then, without being asked, offering the thought of his own accord, he says, "And you ought to release the body, sir, in order to bury him speedily. In dignity. With honor."

Pontius Pilate gapes at the centurion, then at Joseph. He stares back and forth from the fighter to the ruler, from the Roman to the Jew, from the hard man to the soft man, from the poor man to the rich—and he suffers a sort of disorientation because they look alike, these two. Brothers! All at once the supplicants look like brothers.

Pilate is defeated.

He believes this much: that Jesus is dead. He goes this far: to grant the corpse to Joseph.

More than that . . . well, well, he's tired of the whole affair. He's sick to death of a people so completely, so unreasonably, so irredeemably *religious!*

"Go on, get out. Both of you. Go."

They leave together.

† † †

On Maundy Thursday, consider: we *do* bury the living, after all—and often! We bury the living Lord in the graves of ourselves whom he changes, by his indwelling, from tombs to living stones!

This is the persistent gift of the Lord's last supper: that every time we faithfully eat and drink it, Jesus comes within us, and we become his temple here.

Jesus:

Dead, you entered Joseph's tomb
And once, for all, did not exist.
Alive, you enter and commune
Myself in every Eucharist.

For this you mystified the wine,
For this reduced the bread to bone—
To lodge your body, Christ, in mine!
Then here, my Love: come home. Come home.

THE THIRTY-NINTH DAY
GOOD FRIDAY

MARK 15:46

And he bought a linen shroud and, taking him down, wrapped him in the linen shroud and laid him in a tomb which had been hewn out of the rock; and he rolled a stone against the door of the tomb.

Today all times collide. Today all stories are the same. It was a Friday then. It is a Friday now. We call them both by the same preposterous name: Good.

What once was, now—by the mystery of the holy story faithfully and fearfully remembered—is:

Joseph has unrolled a linen cloth and laid it on the ground. It is close-woven and white. It is longer than the human frame and twice as wide. It is a shroud.

He has leaned a ladder to the back side of the cross.

He has climbed the ladder.

Now he draws ropes around the chest, beneath the shoulders of our Lord and over the beam of wood. He throws the loose ends down to the centurion facing him. With a sudden force—and with anguish that there must be force—he wrenches the spikes from the crossbar. The left one: the body of Jesus swings wide away and hangs from one arm. The right: the body slumps. The ropes go taut. The centurion has one in each hand. Joseph whispers, "Wait," descends, then stands below the slouching corpse, below the rain of the dead man's hair. He applies himself to the spike through the heels. The legs drop.

148

"Now," he whispers.

With his left arm he is hugging Jesus at the knees.

"Lower him."

By sad degrees as the Roman pays out rope, the body sinks, shoulders hunched to the ears, Jesus resistless. Joseph receives the torso on his right arm. The head falls back. The mouth opens. The eyes are lidded, blind. The hair rains at Joseph's elbow. Jesus is gaunt. As light as an empty scrip. The body without the sounding breath is light and so pitifully little. Joseph kneels and lays him on the shroud and begins to wind the linen around him for burial.

Somewhere a woman delivers a long, soft, terrible sigh to the world. Who is that?

The door to the tomb is a hole in stone no higher than a human waist. Joseph enters backward, bent down, bearing the shoulders of Jesus. The centurion, on his knees, keeps the legs from dragging dirt.

"Thank you," says Joseph. His voice echoes in the hollow rock. "Thank you. This is enough."

He disposes the body alone, then, and emerges into the darker part of evening. The sun has set. The sky is empty. The air is absolutely still.

There is a descending groove in the stone ledge below the sepulcher's door. Joseph rolls a flat stone down this groove. A single, slow revolution will bring it flush to the hole. No animals will desecrate this body.

There are two sounds in the dusk: the grinding of stone in stone—and once more the soft sigh, a low, compulsive, wordless sigh. Who is that?

Then the door is closed. The deed is done. It is finished.

† † †

That sigh was me, Lord.

That weeper is me, the twentieth century me, attending your burial. Your dying is never far away nor long ago, but always as close as my own. I cry for the sorrow of being at your death.

But I cry also in gratitude that you will be at my death, O my Savior—and that, though I can only cry for yours, you rescue me from mine.

Amen.

THE FORTIETH DAY

HOLY SATURDAY

MARK 15:47

Mary Magdalen and Mary the mother of Joses saw where he was laid.

Stone cold. And the stone is closed. Where do I go from here? Nowhere. Back to the city. Which is a nowhere now. The Master isn't there. The Master is not. Everywhere is nowhere. There's nowhere to go.

What do I do? I don't know what to do. Nothing. The Sabbath has started. So what? So, if I pray I'll be mouthing the sounds. Nothing. And if I pray a vain repetition, what then? Will Heaven be offended? *Well, Heaven has offended me!*

Joseph's stone is like the period that stops the sentence. Boom!—the story's done. And when the story's over, the very air is empty. No place for me. No home for my soul. Silence. Why do I keep standing here? It's dark. It's midnight. Everyone's gone home. Except me. Abandoned. Nothing.

Why can't I leave the tombs?

Because the whole world is a graveyard. Because this is the one that has my Lord.

Jesus! Jesus! Without you I am a nothing in a nowhere! You are dead.

My world is annihilated.

And still—I love you.

† † †

Mary, do this:

Even in your despair, observe the rituals. It is the Sabbath; then let it be the Sabbath after all. Pray your prayers. However hollow and unsatisfying they may feel, God can fill them. God is God, who made the world from nothing—and God as God can still astonish you. He can make of your mouthings a prayer—and of your groanings a hymn. Observe the ritual. Prepare your spices. Return on Sunday, even to this scene of your sorrow, expecting nothing but a corpse, planning nothing but to sigh once more and to pay respects.

One story is done indeed, my Magdalene. You're right. You've entered the dark night of the soul.

But another story—one you cannot conceive of (it's God who conceives it!)—starts at sunrise. And the empty time between, while sadly you prepare the spices, is in fact preparing you! Soon you will change. Soon you will become that holy conundrum which must baffle and antagonize the world: a saint. Saint Mary Magdalene. "As dying, and behold we live; as punished, and yet not killed; as sorrowful, yet always rejoicing; as poor, yet making many rich; as having nothing, and yet possessing all things"—that host of contradictions, the beauty of Spirit, the puzzle of all who know him not, the character of the saints!

Come again on Sunday, Mary, and see how it is that God makes saints.

Come, follow.

THE DAY OF THE RESURRECTION OF OUR LORD

MARK 16:1–8

> And when the Sabbath was past, Mary Magdalene, and Mary the mother of James, and Salome bought spices so that they might go and anoint him.
>
> And very early on the first day of the week they went to the tomb when the sun had risen. And they were saying to one another, "Who will roll away the stone for us from the door of the tomb?" And looking up, they saw that the stone was rolled back. It was very large.
>
> And entering the tomb, they saw a young man sitting on the right side, dressed in a white robe; and they were amazed.
>
> And he said to them, "Do not be amazed. You seek Jesus of Nazareth, who was crucified. He has risen! He is not here. See the place where they laid him. Now go, tell his disciples and Peter that he is going before you to Galilee; there you will see him, as he told you."
>
> And they went out and fled from the tomb; for trembling and astonishment had come upon them; and they said nothing to any one, for they were afraid—

Peter, hold me. Just hold me. I can't stop shaking. Feel it? Hold me tight. I stood in the place where Moses stood, and the world is spinning so fast—

Listen: oils and spices, ointment jars. That's it. Our hands were full, but that's all we carried. Honestly, nothing for ourselves, all for the body of Jesus. Mary and Salome and me. We went outside the city wall. The sun was just rising. Dew on the grass was white, so that we made three trails behind us. And we cast long shadows. There was a sparrow. We wanted to honor Jesus. We were going to touch him. I thought about the smell.

Old Mary was crying.

Suddenly she stopped and said that we were fools, that we couldn't anoint him.

She made me angry.

"Who's going to stop us," I shouted. "Who cares for a criminal's corpse?"

"No," the old woman said, "that's not it. You saw it, too."

"Saw what?"

"The stone. Who will roll the stone from the door?"

"Mary! I will, all right?" I was so mad I really felt I could do it alone. I had seven furies in my breast. I didn't wait. I swept ahead with long strides, raging. Oh, I had such hate for the world and all things and God—

But the stone was rolled back.

No, Peter, listen! This is a very big stone, a very heavy stone, not even you could move it *uphill*, don't you see? But the door of the tomb was open! All my feelings went straight to fear. Something was wrong. I wasn't mad, I was panicking.

I dropped the ointments. I crept forward and went down on my knees and looked inside—

Do you remember what you told me about Moses and Elijah with Jesus on the mountain, and you saw all three of them, and a cloud came, and Jesus grew so bright it blinded you, and the voice of God came down and roared, remember? Peter, I believe you now. And I kiss you, dear friend because of it. I love you so much for telling me that story. O Peter, I know how you felt! I know exactly. It was terror, right? But more than that: fear and love together.

Listen! There was a young man in the tomb, dressed in white like Jesus on the mountain. But not Jesus! Jesus was not there!

This young man knew me. He knew what I was doing there. I never saw him before. He said, "You're looking for Jesus. He has risen."

Peter, are you listening? Do you understand? He said *risen*! I didn't scream.

The man pointed at a stone ledge inside the tomb and said, "He is not here. See the place where they laid him."

I did not scream then—but I stared at the bare ledge and started to shake, and I'll tell you why. Terror. Fear and wonder and love all mixed in me, and my body couldn't take it. Oh, Peter, I still can't take it, but I believe it. I believe it. I stood in the spot where Jesus came back to life. That's so holy! That's so frightening. He isn't the man I thought he was. He is the glory of God! I stood as close to God as Moses did, closer—and I'll tell you why I didn't scream. Because I couldn't even *breathe*. I stared at the stone and I thought how he loved me, how he *loves* me, loves *me*, Peter, plain Mary from Magdala who had seven devils once and no prospects, and it was enough that he loved me so long as he lived, but then he died and it was nothing. But now think, Peter! Think how terribly mighty that love must be to *rise from the dead*! Peter, do you understand what I'm saying to you? This is the love of Almighty God the Father, now, right here! Right here! That's why I'm shaking. Hold me. Hold me. I promise, I'm telling the truth. Hold me tight. Stop my shaking. Peter, believe me—

Well, well, and if you can't believe me, come with me.

The young man in white told me to tell you what to do now, Simon.

Hold me just a little longer, dear, good, and stony Simon. It's a killing terror, isn't it? Exquisite and sharp—a painful, impossible joy. Yes—but I am growing calmer now. Thank you. Here, let me kiss you. And now what?

Why, now we will go and see the Lord alive. And then you will believe me.

For Jesus is going before us to Galilee; there you will see him, exactly as he promised.

† † †

Alleluia!
I see thee, and I do not die!
I see me in thy seeing eye!
As thou art life, in Life am I,
In Love, in Christ and crucified.

Alleluia!
Alleluia!
Alleluia!

Amen.

Preparing for Jesus

Meditations on the Coming of Christ: Advent, Christmas, and the Kingdom

Walter Wangerin Jr.

This is Walter Wangerin's sequel to *Reliving the Passion*, in which he takes the reader, day by day, through the major events and characters leading up to the birth of Jesus. Wangerin contemplates the miracle of Advent, Christmas, and God's Kingdom through the stories of the original characters: Zachariah, Mary, Elizabeth, John the Baptist, Joseph, Jesus himself, Simeon and Anna, and the two kings (not three, as we've always supposed). The characters come alive in classic Wangerin style, and you will see, feel, hear, experience all that they did long ago.

This book is unique because Wangerin looks at Christmas not as the modern holiday it has become but from the perspective of its original happening and its perennial recurrence in our hearts. In addition, the author believes that Christmas does not end on Christmas Day, but is an annual spiritual event that should take place in our souls from December 1 to January 6 (Epiphany) every year. Therefore, his 36 meditations lead the reader from the first glimmers of Jesus' expected arrival, clear through to the visit of the wise kings from the East. The power and beauty and appropriateness of this approach are evident.

Like *Reliving the Passion*, the book has to be experienced to be truly appreciated. It is life-changing.

Hardcover: 978-0-310-20644-6

Share Your Thoughts

With the Author: Your comments will be forwarded to the author when you send them to *zauthor@zondervan.com*.

With Zondervan: Submit your review of this book by writing to *zreview@zondervan.com*.

Free Online Resources at
www.zondervan.com

Zondervan AuthorTracker: Be notified whenever your favorite authors publish new books, go on tour, or post an update about what's happening in their lives at www.zondervan.com/authortracker.

Daily Bible Verses and Devotions: Enrich your life with daily Bible verses or devotions that help you start every morning focused on God. Visit www.zondervan.com/newsletters.

Free Email Publications: Sign up for newsletters on Christian living, academic resources, church ministry, fiction, children's resources, and more. Visit www.zondervan.com/newsletters.

Zondervan Bible Search: Find and compare Bible passages in a variety of translations at www.zondervanbiblesearch.com.

Other Benefits: Register yourself to receive online benefits like coupons and special offers, or to participate in research.